101 Semolina Recipes

(101 Semolina Recipes - Volume 1)

Alice Grady

Copyright: Published in the United States by Alice Grady/ © ALICE GRADY

Published on December, 07 2020

All rights reserved. No part of this publication may be reproduced, stored in retrieval system, copied in any form or by any means, electronic, mechanical, photocopying, recording or otherwise transmitted without written permission from the publisher. Please do not participate in or encourage piracy of this material in any way. You must not circulate this book in any format. ALICE GRADY does not control or direct users' actions and is not responsible for the information or content shared, harm and/or actions of the book readers.

In accordance with the U.S. Copyright Act of 1976, the scanning, uploading and electronic sharing of any part of this book without the permission of the publisher constitute unlawful piracy and theft of the author's intellectual property. If you would like to use material from the book (other than just simply for reviewing the book), prior permission must be obtained by contacting the author at author@shellfishrecipes.com

Thank you for your support of the author's rights.

Content

101 AWESOME SEMOLINA RECIPES 5

1. A Sweet Semolina Saffron Pudding (Sooji Halva) 5
2. Almond Easter Cake With Dates 5
3. April Bloomfield's Ricotta Gnudi 6
4. Atayef Asaferi, Arabic Pancakes 7
5. Balsamic Braised Chicken Thighs 7
6. Basbousa 8
7. Basbousa Semolina Cake Soaked In A Lemon Rosewater Syrup 9
8. Basil And Black Pepper Pappardelle 10
9. Beet Casunziei 10
10. Beetroot Ravioli With Ricotta Cheese Filling&Walnut Butter Sauce 11
11. Blueberry Ricotta Muffins 12
12. Brandied Tropical Fruit Cake 13
13. Breaded And Baked Vidalia Onion Rings With Cornmeal 13
14. Broccoli Rabe, Potato And Rosemary Pizza 14
15. Buckwheat Pasta With Charred Cabbage, Speck, And Provolone 15
16. Butternut Squash And Gorgonzola Tart ... 16
17. Butternut Squash And Roasted Garlic Galette 17
18. Butternut Squash Ravioli With Crispy Sage Butter Sauce 18
19. Cardamom Cookies Aka Naan Khatai 19
20. Carrot Rava Upma 19
21. Carrot Kheer 20
22. Cauliflower Fritters 20
23. Charlotte Druckman's Cacio E Pepe Shortbread 20
24. Cinnamon Tagliatelle With Stracciatella Di Bufula & Spinach 21
25. Coconut Quinoa Pudding 22
26. Crispy Moroccan Pancakes (M'smmen) 23
27. Crème Fraîche Plum Cake With Plum Caramel 23
28. Cuban Bread Inspired Sandwich Rolls 24
29. Cumin Pea And Bulgur Fritters With Lemon Yogurt Sauce 26
30. Cumin Orange Chocolate Semolina Pudding 26
31. Custard Filled Mini Phyllo Cups 27
32. Deconstructed Pesto With A Saute Of Sausage, Peppers, And Onions 27
33. Deep Dish Pizza Dough 28
34. English Muffins 29
35. Fire Roasted Red Pepper Semolina Soup .. 29
36. Fresh Orecciette With Broccoli Rabe, Sausage And Yellow Raisins 30
37. Fried Pickled Celery 31
38. Fried Anchovies With Curry Leaves 32
39. Frito Pie 33
40. Gingerbread Kransecake 33
41. Gnudi 34
42. Grilled Flank Steak Piadina With Cannellini Bean Puree And Arugula 35
43. Gujia Sweet Empanada 36
44. Hand Pulled Breadsticks (Grissini Stirati) .36
45. Homemade Farfalle 37
46. Homemade Pasta With A Lemony Cream, Spinach, And Pea Sauce 38
47. Honeyed Greek Filo Custard 39
48. Hungarian Stuffed Reds With Red Quinoa 40
49. Kale Pizza With Blue Cheese And Walnuts 40
50. Keeping Cake With Middle Eastern Flavors 41
51. Lahm Bi Ajeen 42
52. Lentils Pancake 43
53. MAAMOUL BI FISTOK (PISTACHIO MAAMOUL) 43
54. Ma'moul Cookies Cookies Filled With Date Filling 44
55. Mamool 45
56. Mango Semolina Pudding/ Mango Halwa 46
57. Marak Kubbeh Adom 46
58. Marillenknödeln With Hazelnut Sauce Apricot Dumplings (Austrian) 47
59. Moroccan Crêpes With Spiced Fruit Compote 48
60. Mozzarella, Prosciutto And Olive Salad Stromboli 49
61. ORANGE PATISHAPTA (The Pancake Stuffed With Coconut And Brown Sugar) 51
62. Orange Cake (Portokalopita) 51
63. PALLAPPAM (Crisp Laced Rice Pancakes)

	52	
64.	PINEAPPLE HALWA	52
65.	Pasta E Roveja	53
66.	Patishapta Indian Crepe With Cardamom Coconut Filling, Drizzled With Date Syrup	53
67.	Peach & Tomato Summer Pie	54
68.	Pici Con Le Briciole (Pici With Breadcrumbs)	55
69.	Pizza Rustica	56
70.	Pizza With Butternut Squash Sauce	56
71.	Revani, Syrup Soaked Semolina Cake	57
72.	Ricotta Gnocchi Served With Blueberry Compote	58
73.	Ricotta Feta Gnocchi Tossed In Maple Brown Butter And Sweet Peas Sauce	59
74.	Roasted Carrot Soup With Meyer Lemon And Rosemary	59
75.	Rye Orecchiette With Stinging Nettles, Sheep's Milk Feta, And Chive Blossoms	60
76.	SCALLION PANCAKE WITH PEANUT COCONUT TAMARIND CHUTNEY	61
77.	SEMOLINA WITH TOASTED SEEDS AND VEGETABLES	62
78.	SEMOLINA YOGURT ROSE PETAL CAKE/ROSE FLAVOURED BASBOUSA	63
79.	SUJI HALWA	63
80.	Sardinian Clam Stew With Fregola	64
81.	Savory Vegetable Cake	65
82.	Semolina Crackers With Baked On Goat Cheese	66
83.	Semolina Dumplings	66
84.	Semolina Pancakes With Spicy Merguez Filling	67
85.	Sesame Semolina Pancakes	68
86.	Sfogliatelle	68
87.	Sfoof Vegan Lebanese Yellow Tea Cake	70
88.	Skinny Dip Squash (Butternut Gnudi)	71
89.	Soda Bread With Walnuts And Rolled Oats	72
90.	Sooji Ka Halwa (A Sweet Made From Semolina)	72
91.	Springtime Asparagus And Ricotta Pizza	73
92.	Sri Lankan Christmas Cake	74
93.	Stinging Nettle Pasta	75
94.	Summer Squash With Saffron Fettuccine	75
95.	Trick To Rolling Out Homemade Pasta Dough!	76
96.	Vegetable Stuffed Snack Cakes	77
97.	Vermicelli And Semolina Idli	78
98.	Weeknight Margeritesque Pizza	78
99.	Zapekanka, A Classic Breakfast Dish From Russian Cuisine	79
100.	Roasted Semolina Soup	80
101.	Semolina With Red Fruit Topping	80

INDEX 82

CONCLUSION 85

101 Awesome Semolina Recipes

***

1. A Sweet Semolina Saffron Pudding (Sooji Halva)

Serving: Makes about 4 cups | Prep: | Cook: | Ready in:

Ingredients

- 1 stick of butter, unsalted
- 1 cup semolina
- 1 cup sugar
- 3 cups water
- 1 pinch saffron
- 10 green cardamom pods (crushed and muddled, discard the shells, use the seeds)*
- 15 pistachios (crushed)*
- 15 raw almonds (slivered)*
- *save some of each to use as a garnish

Direction

- In a medium/large saucepan, on low heat, slowly melt together the butter and semolina. Stir occasionally and mix well, until the mixture is golden/dark brown. (This should take about 20 minutes).
- At the same time, in a separate small/medium sized saucepan, on medium/low, heat the sugar, water, saffron and cardamom seeds. Heat well, so the sugar dissolves (boiling is okay but not necessary).
- When the sugar has dissolved and the semolina is brown, carefully add the sugar water to the semolina (it may bubble a lot, turn the heat down if necessary). Stir well.
- Stir in most of the almonds and pistachios (reserving some to use as a garnish). Keep stirring and cooking on low for about 7-10 minutes, (until all of the water is absorbed and the surface areas that have contact with the pan get smooth).
- Enjoy served warm and topped with the remaining crushed pistachios, slivered almonds and crushed cardamom seeds.

2. Almond Easter Cake With Dates

Serving: Makes 1 pie | Prep: | Cook: | Ready in:

Ingredients

- 200g flour
- 1 pinch salt
- 125g cold butter
- 3 tablespoons sugar
- 1/2 lemon, zest and juice
- 400 milliliters almond soy milk
- 1 pinch salt
- 4 tablespoons semolina
- 50g butter
- 3 tablespoons sugar
- 3 tablespoons ground almonds
- 3 tablespoons chopped dates
- 1 packet vanilla sugar
- 1 tablespoon baking powder
- 3 tablespoons soy flour

Direction

- For the dough: stir together 200g flour, salt and 125g cold butter. Add lemon zest and sugar and knead everything together by hand. Form a ball and chill in the refrigerator for 30 minutes
- For the filling, heat the soymilk and salt, stir in semolina. Cook for 10-20 minutes on low heat, stirring occasionally with a whisk
- Preheat oven on 420F
- Remove soymilk from heat and add the butter to let it melt. Now add lemon juice, sugar,

ground almonds, dates, vanilla sugar, baking powder. Stir well to combine.
- Grease a round pie pan. Roll out the dough on the bottom and sides (1.5 inches). Prick the bottom of the dough with a fork. Pour in the filling
- Bake for 20-30 minutes. Let cool before serving

3. April Bloomfield's Ricotta Gnudi

Serving: Serves 4 to 6 as an appetizer (16 to 20 gnudi) | Prep: | Cook: |Ready in:

Ingredients

- For the gnudi:
- 16 ounces great-quality ricotta (sheep or cow)
- 2 ounces Parmesan cheese, finely grated, plus more for garnishing
- Freshly ground black pepper
- Salt
- 4 cups fine semolina flour (sometimes sold as sooji), divided
- For the butter sauces and serving.
- 6 tablespoons unsalted butter, divided
- 12 to 15 sage leaves

Direction

- For the gnudi:
- Line a large plate with several layers of paper towels or a clean kitchen towel. Transfer the ricotta to the towels and spread it out with a spatula or the back of a spoon. Place more layers of paper towels (or an additional dish towel) over top and press down firmly with your hands to blot excess moisture. Peel off the towels.
- Weigh out 12 ounces of ricotta. (Reserve any leftovers for another use.) Scrape into a bowl, then add the grated Parmesan and season heavily with black pepper (if desired). Season with salt, taste, and adjust. Transfer to a clean plate, spread into a thin layer, and freeze for 15 minutes.
- Meanwhile, pour half the semolina flour into a large bowl and the other into a 9- by 13-inch baking dish.
- Scrape the chilled ricotta mixture into a bowl and fold with a spatula so that no frozen chunks remain. Use a small cookie scoop or a spoon to form a ball of ricotta about 1 1/2 inches wide (2 tablespoons). Transfer to the bowl with the semolina, then use your fingers to cover it with semolina flour. Pick up the ball, roll it into a neat sphere with your hands, and then nestle into the 9 by 13. Repeat until all the ricotta's been used—you should have between 16 and 20 gnudi.
- Cover the dish with plastic wrap, then put it in the fridge for 3 days, turning once a day. At the end of 3 days, you can cook the gnudi or you can freeze them. (Remove from the semolina, then freeze on a baking sheet until solid, about 1 hour, before transferring to a freezer bag for up to 2 months. When you want to cook them, thaw them overnight in the refrigerator on a plate covered with plastic wrap.)
- If you're making the butter sauces, skip to the directions below.
- To cook the gnudi, bring a large pot of well-salted water to a boil. Add the gnudi and cook, stirring very gently, for about 3 minutes. Then use a slotted spoon to transfer the gnudi to plates or follow the steps below if you'd like to make the butter sauces.
- For the butter sauces and serving.
- For the brown butter sauce, heat 2 tablespoons of butter in a medium saucepan over medium-low heat until foaming subsides, the butter solids have turned golden brown, and the butter smells nutty. Add sage leaves, season lightly with salt, and cook, flipping the leaves occasionally, until crisp, about 2 minutes. Using tongs, transfer the leaves to a plate lined with paper towels to drain. Pour the brown butter into a bowl.
- As you bring the water for the gnudi to a boil, place the 4 tablespoons remaining butter in a

medium skillet. Transfer the cooked gnudi to the skillet with a slotted spoon, making sure to bring plenty of their cooking liquid with them, place over high heat, and shake and stir gently so that the butter and pasta water emulsify into a creamy sauce, about 1 minute. Season with salt to taste.
- Transfer gnudi and their sauce to serving plates. Top with fried sage leaves and a drizzle of brown butter. Sprinkle with additional grated Parmesan and freshly ground black pepper.

4. Atayef Asaferi, Arabic Pancakes

Serving: Serves 4-6 | Prep: | Cook: | Ready in:

Ingredients

- For the Dough
- 1 cup All purpose flour
- 1/4 cup Semolina flour
- 1/4   Active dry yeast
- 1/2 teaspoon Baking powder (may need more, see instructions)
- 1 tablespoon Sugar
- 1 tablespoon Vegetable oil
- 1 1/2 cups Warm water (may need more, see instructions)
- For the Filling
- 3 cups Ricotta cheese
- 3/4 teaspoon Ground cinnamon
- 3/4 teaspoon Ground Cardamon
- 2/3 cup Crushed pistachios

Direction

- To cook the atayef: 1. In a large bowl, mix together all-purpose flour, semolina flour, yeast, baking powder, and sugar. Add in vegetable oil and water and whisk until mixture is thin and clump-free. Allow the batter to rest for 10 minutes. 2. Heat a non-stick pan over medium heat. Once pan is hot, add 1 tablespoon of batter to center. You should bubbles form around the edges and then spread to the entire surface. If the bubbles don't spread, your batter is too thick. Add 2 tablespoons of water to the batter, whisk, and try again. If you add water and get the same result the second time, try adding ½ a teaspoon of baking powder, whisk, and try again. You should now see bubbles forming across your entire atayef. 3. Your atayef is done cooking when it is no longer shiny and the bottom has browned evenly, about 1-2 minutes. Transfer atayef to a clean kitchen towel and cover to keep in moisture (and make it easy to seal). Continue to make remaining atayef until batter runs out. Layer atayef on kitchen towel with like sides facing each other (bubbly side touches bubbly side of next atayef, cooked sides touches cooked side, etc.).
- To stuff the atayef: 4. In a medium bowl, mix together ricotta, ground cinnamon, and ground cardamom. Pour crushed pistachios into a shallow bowl or small plate. 5. To stuff, fold the atayef in a half circle and pinch along the sides, stopping halfway up. Use a small spoon to scoop ricotta mixture into the opening, then dip atayef into pistachios.6. Serve with a drizzle of maple syrup.
- Recipe adapted from Chef in Disguise.

5. Balsamic Braised Chicken Thighs

Serving: Serves 4 | Prep: | Cook: | Ready in:

Ingredients

- INGREDIENTS (for braising liquid)
- 1 1/2 cups Proseco (you could also use sparkling wine or vermouth)
- 1 cup chicken stock
- 1/4 cup balsamic vinegar
- 2 tablespoons lemon juice (approximately juice of 1/2 lemon)

- 1 tablespoon fig paste
- 1 tablespoon honey
- 2 tablespoons Dijon mustard
- 1 tablespoon chicken Demi-glacé (if solid, cut a 1/2" x 3/4" chunk)
- 1 tablespoon chopped fresh rosemary
- 2-3 pieces Balinese Long Peppers (optional) long peppers are very fragrant but not a typical ingredient. I have a box in my pantry that I got several years ago from a specialty food store. I use them when I want to add an exotic flavor that is not over powering
- INGREDIENTS (for chicken)
- 1 1/2 - 2 pounds INGREDIENTS (for chicken) (approximately 8 thighs)
- Sea salt and fresh ground pepper for seasoning
- 1/4 cup semolina flour
- 2 tablespoons olive oil for saluting
- 2 sweet onions, skin peeled, cut into 1/4 each slices
- 12-16 small baby Dutch potatoes, rinsed
- 2 Belgium endives, rinsed
- 1 teaspoon natural sugar
- natural sugar

Direction

- INGREDIENTS (for braising liquid)
- PREP braising liquid. Add all the ingredients to a small saucepan and bring to a light boil.
- Reduce the heat and let simmer, uncovered, until the flavors meld (approximately 10 minutes).
- INGREDIENTS (for chicken)
- PREP chicken. Rinse and pat dry the chicken thighs.
- Season chicken with sea salt and pepper. Sprinkle the semolina flour over to coat thighs, shaking off excess.
- Heat a large, heavy bottomed, Dutch oven with low sides until hot. Add the olive oil and brown the chicken thighs on one side. Turn the thighs over, cook for one minute then add in the onions. Be sure that the onions end up slightly under the chicken. Pour over the braising liquid then add the potatoes, pushing them to submerge in the liquid.
- Bring the liquid to a simmer and transfer to a 375 degree oven (not covered). Baste every 15 minutes for approximately an hour.
- After 45 minutes, add the Belgium endives and let cook for 5 minutes or until just tender. Remove and cut them in half lengthwise. Set aside
- When the chicken is done tender and nicely browned (typically after one hour cooking time), remove the pan from the oven, cover and let rest for 10 minutes while you finish the endive.
- To finish the endive, heat a sauté pan to hot. Sprinkle the sugar over the bottom of the pan and set the endive in cut side down. Allow this to sit, undisturbed for a few minutes as it caramelizes. Sprinkle with sea salt and fresh pepper. Squeeze in the lemon juice.
- PLATE: Divide the potatoes and onions among four plates. Top, slightly askew, with one or two thighs. Put one endive half alongside. Spoon the sauce over the chicken or in front on the plate, garnish.

6. Basbousa

Serving: Serves 16 | Prep: | Cook: |Ready in:

Ingredients

- FOR CAKE BATTER
- 1/2 cup All-Purpose Flour
- 3/4 cup Vegetable Oil
- 1 Egg
- 1 teaspoon Vanilla Extract
- 1 1/2 cups Semolina
- 1 cup Milk
- 1/2 cup Sugar
- 1 teaspoon Baking Powder
- FOR SUGAR SYRUP
- 1 cup Sugar
- 1 cup Water

- 1/4 Lemon juice

Direction

- SUGAR SYRUP-Bring water, sugar, and half lemon juice to boil till all the sugar gets dissolved in the water or until string consistency.
- Cool the sugar syrup to room temp and store in a glass jar.
- Blanch some almonds and keep aside dry.
- Take a large bowl and mix all the dry ingredients.
- Add the veg oil and milk and combine the mixture well with a spatula.
- Now whisk an egg and vanilla essence into the above mixture. Mix well.
- Pour this cake mixture into the greased pan.
- Score lines on the mixture with a knife and makes a pattern.
- Bake @ 350 deg F for 30 mins.
- Take the pan out and cut right through the scored lines on the cake.
- Pour the cold sugar syrup onto the hot cake.
- Back into the oven for another 15 mins.
- Cool the cake to room temp or serve warm.
- Tip# you can use fine and coarse semolina in equal parts for the recipe. Tip# Substitute sugar syrup with thickened milk mixture (Milkmaid + Heavy cream) for a fudgy semolina cake.

7. Basbousa Semolina Cake Soaked In A Lemon Rosewater Syrup

Serving: Serves 4 to 6 | Prep: | Cook: |Ready in:

Ingredients

- For the Cake
- 3/4 cup semolina
- 1/2 cup all purpose flour
- 1 teaspoon baking powder
- 1 egg
- 4 tablespoons softened butter
- 1/2 cup whole milk yogurt
- 2 tablespoons sugar
- Almonds to garnish
- For the syrup
- 3/4 cup water
- 1/2 cup sugar
- 2 limes
- 1 tablespoon freshly grated citrus zest (lemon, lime and or orange)
- 1 teaspoon rosewater

Direction

- Mix in the semolina, flour and the baking powder and stir well.
- Mix in the egg, butter and yogurt and the sugar and mix well with either a strong wooden spoon or an electric beater until well mixed. Do not overbeat.
- Grease a glass casserole and pour in the mixture.
- Place the almonds about 2 inches apart, to essentially ensure a placement that is right in the center, when cut into squares.
- Cover with the cling wrap and microwave for 5 minutes on high. This does depend on your microwave, I recommend, doing this first for 3 minutes and then adding 2 more until the mixture is firm, but not too dry.
- While this is cooking, place the water and the sugar on the stovetop, heat till the sugar is dissolved and the mixture comes to a boil.
- Reduce the heat and simmer for 10 minutes.
- Cut the limes and squeeze in the juice and stir in the zest.
- Add in the rosewater.
- Cut the semolina mixture into 2 inch squares, such that the almonds are in the center.
- Pour over the syrup, this will first seem like a lot but eventually it get absorbed. Let it soak for at least 30 minutes and serve warm.

8. Basil And Black Pepper Pappardelle

Serving: Serves 6-8 depending on serving size | Prep: | Cook: | Ready in:

Ingredients

- 1 3/4 cups all purpose flour
- 1 cup semolina
- 1/2 teaspoon kosher salt
- 4-6 turns of pepper mill
- 6 large eggs at room temperature
- 1 tablespoon olive oil
- handful fresh basil cleaned and torn
- 2 tablespoons water

Direction

- To the food processor add the flours, salt and pepper and pulse once. Lightly beat your eggs in measuring cup, add olive oil, water and basil. Turn machine on and pour the egg and basil through the feeding tube, turn machine off when dough comes together. Empty onto floured work surface. Knead the dough until it becomes smooth and elastic, Divide the dough into two balls, flatten slightly and wrap each in plastic wrap. Let rest for at least an hour up to overnight in the refrigerator. If making lesser amount of pasta one of the disks of dough can be frozen.
- On floured work surface roll out your dough starting from the middle of the ball and working outward. Roll into a square shape as thinly as possible, it takes some work to get the dough into a thin square, make sure it's thin enough that when lifted you can see your finger through the dough. Sprinkle with semolina and loosely roll into a cylinder, slice 3/4 inch thick pieces, open them and lay on sheet pan on parchment and toss with more semolina, lay loosely on pan and let them sit uncovered for 10 minutes. Cook in large pot of salted boiling water

9. Beet Casunziei

Serving: Makes about 24 ravioli, enough for two people | Prep: 0hours0mins | Cook: 0hours0mins | Ready in:

Ingredients

- Pasta dough (straight from the Four Seasons)
- 1 1/2 cups unbleached, all purpose flour
- 2 medium eggs
- 1/4 cup water
- 2 tablespoons olive oil
- Salt
- For the filling, sauce, and assembly
- 2 cups cooked, peeled, and diced red beet (about 1 large beet)
- 1 cup fresh ricotta
- 1/4 cup grated Parmigiano Reggiano
- 2 tablespoons chopped parsley
- 1 tablespoon chopped thyme
- Salt, to taste
- Semolina flour or fine cornmeal, for prepping the casunsei
- 1 egg, for assembling pasta
- 1 stick of butter
- 2 tablespoons poppy seeds

Direction

- Pasta dough (straight from the Four Seasons)
- Mound the flour on a board and make a well in the center. Drop the eggs and the water into the well.
- Using a fork, gently break up the eggs and start to incorporate the flour from around the inside of the well.
- When the dough begins to thicken, use a bench scraper to lift and fold the dough over, incorporating more flour a little at a time until you have a dough that is easy to knead. By the time you've incorporated about half the flour, you should be able to change your technique, kneading the dough with your hands until it all comes together in a mass.
- Continue kneading until you have a smooth, compact dough, rubbing the outside with the olive oil and kneading it in. If the dough seems

too dry, dip your hands in water and knead again—this will add just a touch of moisture. On the other hand, if the dough seems too wet, add a sprinkle of flour and knead to combine.
- Set the dough aside, covered in plastic wrap, for at least 15 minutes. At this point, you may also refrigerate the wrapped dough for up to 6 hours, being sure to bring it back to room temperature before rolling it again.
- For the filling, sauce, and assembly
- To make the filling: Purée the beets, ricotta, cheese, parsley, thyme, and salt (to taste) in a food processor or blender until combined.
- To make the casunsei: Fill a pastry bag with the beet filling and sprinkle a sheet tray with a layer of semolina flour or fine cornmeal.
- Beginning with half the pasta dough (and keeping the other half covered), roll out the dough on a lightly floured board to make a long rectangle, about 27 inches long and 4 inches wide.
- Pipe dabs of filling, about a tablespoon each and 1/2-inch apart, in a regular line down the length of the sheet. Don't put the dabs in the center of the sheet—rather, keep them towards the bottom so that you can fold the top half of the sheet over them. You should be able to get at least 18 dabs on the first sheet of pasta.
- Break the egg into a small bowl and beat in about 1/4 cup of water, then brush this mixture along the edges and in between each of the dabs of filling.
- Fold the top half over all the way along, pressing down with the side of your hand along the edges and in between each of the filling dabs to make a series of 18 ravioli, approximately 1 1/2 by 2 inches, each one filled with beet purée.
- Use a round pasta cutter to stamp them out, making sure that each one is sealed well.
- Carefully, pick up the ravioli and gently lay them, one by one, on the prepared tray. Do not allow them to touch overlap. If you're not going to cook them right away, cover them with a dry kitchen towel.
- Repeat with the remaining pasta dough.

- To make the dish and sauce: Get a pot of pasta water on to boil—many people believe in salting the water when it comes to a boil but I always salt it ahead of time so I don't forget.
- Meanwhile, melt the butter in a pan on gentle heat and add the poppy seeds to gently toast, being sure not to let the butter brown. Remove from heat.
- When the water is boiling, tip the casunsei gently into the pot. The pasta should float when cooked.
- Gently scoop them out with a slotted spoon as ready, draining as much water off them as you can.
- Carefully lay them in the pan with the melted butter, letting the butter and poppy seeds coat the casunsei before placing them in a serving bowl or individual plates. Drizzle any remaining butter over them and eat immediately.

10. Beetroot Ravioli With Ricotta Cheese Filling&Walnut Butter Sauce

Serving: Serves 4 | Prep: | Cook: | Ready in:

Ingredients

- Dough
- 200 grams flour
- 50 grams semolina
- 80 grams beet puree
- 2 eggs
- 1 tablespoon olive oil
- 5 grams salt
- Filling
- 200 grams beetroot
- 200 grams ricotta cheese
- 30 grams parmesan
- 1/4 lemon zest
- 1 pinch nutmeg
- 2 tablespoons chopped parsley
- 1 tablespoon honey

- salt&blackpepper
- 30 grams butter
- 20 grams ground walnut
- 1 sprig fresh thyme
- 1/4 orange zest
- 2 tablespoons orange juice
- salt&pepper

Direction

- Wash beetroots with a brush. Place them in tin foil and bake them at 180C until soft for about 45-55 minutes.
- For the dough squeeze the juice of a fresh beetroot and make a puree. Mound the flour and semolina on a clean work surface and create a well in the center. Place the puree, eggs and oil in the center. Using a fork, whisk together and slowly start dragging the flour into the mixture. Add this to the dry ingredients. Knead until all are well combined and the dough is smooth and elastic, about 10 minutes. Add more juice or flour to adjust the consistency of the dough. Put in a cling film and rest in the fridge for about 30-45 minutes.
- Take the beetroots out the oven and let them cool. Peel and grate the beetroots adding ricotta and honey. Add toasted breadcrumbs, nutmeg, lemon zest & juice, salt, pepper and grated parmesan.
- Set up a pasta machine and turn it to the largest opening. Cut off pieces of dough about the size of an egg. Working with one piece of dough at a time, roll the dough into sheets about 3-4mm thick. Lay one pasta sheet flat on a lightly floured work surface and determine approximately where the halfway point is lengthwise. Use a pastry brush to lightly wet one half of the dough with water. Spoon mounds of the filling, about 2 teaspoons each, onto half of the wet side of the dough, leaving about a 1-1.5 cm between the mounds. Fold the dry half of the sheet over lengthwise to cover the filling.
- Press the pasta sheets together to seal the edges around the filling, and press out any excess air. Use a pastry cutter or knife to cut individual ravioli. As you cut out the ravioli, place them on a plate or baking sheet sprinkled with flour to keep them from sticking. Repeat with the remaining pasta and filling.
- Bring a large pot of salted water to a boil. Add the ravioli all at once and stir a few times to submerge and separate them. Cook, uncovered, at a gentle boil until the pasta is just tender to the bite, 2 to 3 minutes. Drain the ravioli thoroughly.
- For the sauce, add butter in a pan, cook until slightly brown, add grated walnuts, orange zest and juice. Serve the raviolis with the sauce and sprinkle fresh thyme on top.

11. Blueberry Ricotta Muffins

Serving: Serves 4 | Prep: | Cook: |Ready in:

Ingredients

- 2 Eggs
- 1 cup Ricotta
- 1 teaspoon Baking powder
- 5 tablespoons Maple syrup
- 1 Lemon
- 1 1/2 tablespoons Butter
- 1 cup Semolina
- 1 handful Blueberries

Direction

- 1. Preheat oven to 360 F.
- 2. Using an electric mixer or a whisk beat the eggs until slightly foamy (1-3 minutes).
- 3. Add ricotta, 4 tablespoons of maple syrup, baking powder, 1 teaspoon of grated lemon zest, 1 tablespoon of lemon juice, and semolina. Mix.
- 4. Cut the cold butter into little tiny chunks and mix them into the muffin batter.
- 5. Add fresh blueberries and mix.
- 6. Pour the muffin batter into the muffin-shaped baking dish.

- 7. Dip 4 thin round lemon slices into the maple syrup and place them on top of the muffins.
- 8. Bake the muffins for 30-35 minutes.
- 9. Take the muffins out and let them cool down for a few minutes.
- Enjoy your breakfast!

12. Brandied Tropical Fruit Cake

Serving: Makes two 13x9 inch cake pans | Prep: | Cook: | Ready in:

Ingredients

- 6 ounces almonds, finely chopped
- 6 ounces macadamia nuts, finely chopped
- 10 ounces candied mango
- 10 ounces sultanas
- 8 ounces candied papaya
- 8 ounces candied cherries
- 8 ounces candied cantaloupe
- 8 ounces candied lemon peel
- 8 ounces candied ginger
- 8 ounces candied orange peel
- 10 ounces butter
- 10 ounces semolina
- 16 egg yolks
- 8 egg whites
- 6 ounces granulated sugar
- Zest of one lemon, finely shredded
- Zest of one orange, finely shredded
- Juice of one orange
- Juice of half lemon
- 2 tablespoons rose water
- 2 tablespoons vanilla extract
- 1 teaspoon allspice
- 1 1/2 cups rum, (plus more for drizzling)

Direction

- Chop the nuts, sultanas and candied fruits into small pieces. Add the orange juice, lemon juice, brandy and half of the rose water and vanilla extract. Mix well and leave in a jar for a day.
- Beat the butter and sugar until creamy. Beat in the egg yolks. Add the orange zest, lemon zest and remaining rose water and vanilla extract, and continue to beat until combined. Add the semolina and allspice and mix until well combined.
- Transfer the batter to a large bowl, add the brandied fruit mixture, and stir well until fruits and nuts are dispersed evenly throughout the batter.
- But the egg whites until stiff. Gently fold the whites into the cake batter.
- Preheat the oven to 250F. Prepare two 13x9 inch cake pans. (If using non-stick pans, line with parchment paper.). Turn the batter into the pans and bake for about 2 ½ - 3 hours.
- When done, remove the cake from the oven. Let it cool in the pan for about 30min and then remove from the pan.
- Drizzle the cake with additional brandy and let it cool completely. Wrap the cake tightly in aluminum foil and store for at least a week before serving. (The cake gets better as it ages, and my optimal aging time is 8-12 weeks. The cake can be kept for a year in an airtight container. And you can keep on drizzling the brandy to keep it moist!)

13. Breaded And Baked Vidalia Onion Rings With Cornmeal

Serving: Serves 16 | Prep: | Cook: | Ready in:

Ingredients

- Nonstick olive oil spray
- 3 cups fine semolina flour
- 2 tablespoons ancho chili powder
- 4 teaspoons salt, divided
- 8 cups panko breadcrumbs
- 2 tablespoons chipotle chili powder
- 4 large eggs
- 4 large sweet onions, such as Vidalia or Walla Walla, peeled

Direction

- Preheat oven to 425°F. Spray two baking sheets with nonstick olive oil spray, line them with parchment paper, and spray with another coating of olive oil spray.
- Combine the semolina, ancho powder, and two teaspoons salt in a shallow, flat-bottomed bowl and stir gently to combine.
- In another shallow, flat-bottomed bowl, combine the eggs and ¼ cup water and beat lightly.
- In a third shallow, flat-bottomed bowl, combine the panko breadcrumbs, chipotle powder, and the remaining two teaspoons salt, and stir gently to combine. Line up the bowls in a row and place them next to the baking sheets.
- Cut the onions into ⅓- to ½-inch slices. Do not break the rings apart. You'll have about 8 slices per onion.
- Holding one slice of onion gently so that the rings do not break, place the slice flat in the semolina, and pat some of the mixture on the top to coat the entire slice very well.
- Still holding the onion slice together, transfer it to the egg mixture and coat it with egg.
- Transfer the onion slice to the panko mixture and coat well, patting panko liberally and thoroughly on top (but not between the rings).
- Place the onion on the prepared baking sheet. Repeat with the remaining onion slices and place on the sheet about one inch apart from each other. Bake for 10 to 12 minutes, or until crunchy. These are best served immediately.

14. Broccoli Rabe, Potato And Rosemary Pizza

Serving: Serves 2 10" pizzas or 4 mini-pizzas | Prep: 0hours0mins | Cook: 0hours0mins | Ready in:

Ingredients

- Broccoli Rabe, Potato and Rosemary Pizza
- 2 uncooked pizza crusts (recipe below)
- 1 large yukon gold potato, very thinly sliced
- Salt
- Extra-virgin olive oil
- 1/2 pound broccoli rabe, washed, ends trimmed
- 1 large garlic clove, minced, plus 2 garlic cloves lightly smashed but still intact
- 1/4 teaspoon crushed red pepper flakes
- 8 ounces fresh mozzarella cheese, thinly sliced
- 2 tablespoons fresh rosemary leaves
- 1/2 cup finely grated Pecorino Romano cheese
- Freshly ground black pepper
- Rosemary sprigs for garnish
- Pizza Dough Recipe
- 2 teaspoons dry yeast
- 1/2 cup lukewarm water
- 3 1/2 cups all-purpose flour
- 1/4 cup semolina flour
- 1 teaspoon salt
- 3/4 cup cold water
- 1/4 cup olive oil

Direction

- Broccoli Rabe, Potato and Rosemary Pizza
- Preheat oven to 375 F.
- Toss potatoes with 1 tablespoon olive oil and 1 teaspoon salt in a large bowl. Arrange potatoes in one layer on a baking tray. Bake until edges begin to turn golden brown, 15 to 20 minutes. Remove from oven and let cool. Increase oven temperature to 475 F.
- Bring a large pot of salted water to boil. Add broccoli rabe and blanch 30 seconds; drain. Plunge broccoli rabe into a bowl of ice water. Cool and drain again. Lay in one layer on a kitchen towel to thoroughly dry. Cut in 2" pieces.
- Heat one tablespoon olive oil in skillet over medium heat. Add minced garlic and red pepper flakes. Sauté briefly, 30 seconds. Add broccoli rabe and 1/2 teaspoon salt. Sauté one minute. Remove from heat. Taste and add more salt if necessary.

- Assemble pizzas: Lightly brush pizza crusts with olive oil. Rub all over with smashed garlic cloves.
- Arrange one layer mozzarella cheese over crusts. Top with one layer of potatoes and broccoli rabe. Sprinkle one tablespoon rosemary over each crust. Top with grated Pecorino cheese.
- Bake on pizza stone or on tray on lowest rack in oven until crust is golden brown and cheese is bubbly, about 15 minutes.
- Before serving, sprinkle with freshly ground black pepper. Garnish with fresh rosemary leaves and drizzle with extra-virgin olive oil.
- Pizza Dough Recipe
- Stir yeast and lukewarm water together in a bowl. Add 1/4 cup all-purpose flour and semolina. Mix well. Let sit until bubbly, about 30 minutes.
- Combine remaining flour and salt in another bowl. Add to yeast with cold water and olive oil. Mix well to form a dough.
- Turn dough out onto a lightly floured board and knead with hands until dough is smooth and elastic, about 10 minutes. Or use a mixer with a dough hook, and knead about 5 minutes.
- Place dough in a lightly oiled bowl and turn to coat all sides with oil. Cover bowl loosely with plastic wrap. Let rise in a warm place until doubled in size, 1 to 2 hours. Punch dough down, and let rise another 45 minutes.
- Divide dough into 2 equal disks (or 4 if you would like small pizzas.) Let rest 30 minutes before shaping. Lightly flour a work surface. Using your fingers or heels of your hands, stretch the disks out to 10" shapes.

15. Buckwheat Pasta With Charred Cabbage, Speck, And Provolone

Serving: Serves 4 | Prep: | Cook: | Ready in:

Ingredients

- 1 cup buckwheat flour
- 1/2 cup Italian OO flour (or substitute all-purpose flour), plus extra for rolling
- 3 whole eggs, plus 1 extra yolk
- 1/2 head savoy cabbage
- Grapeseed oil (or substitute canola or vegetable oil)
- 1 tablespoon caraway seeds, lightly crushed in a mortar and pestle or spice grinder
- Zest of 1 lemon
- Juice of 1/2 a lemon
- Salt
- 1 cup semolina flour, to be used for rolling
- 6 tablespoons butter
- 3 cloves garlic, thinly sliced
- 1 teaspoon chile flakes
- 1/2 pound aged provolone
- 1/8 pound speck, cut into thin strips

Direction

- Add the two types of flour to a large mixing bowl, and whisk to combine. Form a well in the center of the flour. Make the flour look like a volcano. Add the eggs and extra yolk to the center of the flour volcano. Using a fork, beat the eggs in the center of the flour, and gradually incorporate more flour from the periphery. When about two thirds of the flour has been incorporated into the eggs, I like to use my bare hands to push the remaining flour into the wet dough mixture and form a ball of dough. You can also just keep using the fork.
- Remove the wet dough ball from the mixing bowl and place it on a good kneading surface (a table, counter, cutting board, whatever works). Wash your hands. You don't want stray clumps of dry crumbly dough getting incorporated into your nice dough. Set yourself up with a small bowl of extra OO flour to be used as bench flour. Knead the dough for approximately 10 minutes. The better you knead the dough now, the easier it will be to roll it out later. If the dough feels too tacky and sticks to your hands, liberally dust it with bench flour. (Don't worry if you need to repeatedly add extra bench flour.) After 10

minutes of kneading, the dough should feel smooth and pliable. Wrap it in plastic wrap and let it rest at room temperature for 30 minutes.

- While the dough is resting, turn your attention to the savoy cabbage. Remove the core, and cut the cabbage into 1 inch squares. Set a large skillet over high heat, and add just enough grapeseed oil to cover the bottom of the skillet. When the oil begins to lightly smoke, add the cabbage. Watch out, it might splatter. You want to cook the cabbage in a single, even layer, so you will likely have to cook the cabbage in batches. Toss the cabbage in the skillet. When it is wilted and slightly charred, after approximately 2 minutes, remove it from the pan. When all of the cabbage is cooked, season it with the crushed caraway seeds, lemon zest, lemon juice, and salt to taste. Set the cabbage aside.
- Roll out your pasta: Depending on how much room you have to work with, you should probably divide the dough into two or three balls, and work in batches, rolling out one ball at a time and keeping the rest of the dough covered in plastic wrap. Set your pasta roller to the widest setting, and pass the dough through. If it feels tacky, sprinkle it with semolina flour. Fold the dough over on itself in half, and pass it through the widest setting again. Repeat this step until the dough looks smooth and is shaped like a rectangle. Adjust the pasta roller so that it is one notch thinner, and pass the dough through. Continue passing the dough on incrementally smaller settings. When you have passed the dough through the second-thinnest setting, you're done. Using a pasta cutter, cut the dough into 1 inch squares the shape of a handkerchief. Dust a parchment-lined rimmed baking sheet with semolina flour, and transfer the handkerchief pasta to the baking sheet. Top with extra semolina so that it doesn't stick to itself. You can make the pasta ahead of time and store it in the freezer.
- Set a large pot of water over high heat and bring the water to a boil. While you are waiting for the water to boil, set a large skillet over medium heat. Add the butter. When it is melted, add the garlic and the chili flakes. Cook until the garlic just begins to brown. Turn off the heat.
- When the water is boiling, add salt so that the water tastes like the ocean. Add the pasta and cook until it floats to the surface, approximately 1 to 2 minutes. Drain the pasta, reserving 1/4 cup of pasta water. Add the cooked pasta and the reserved pasta water to the skillet with the garlic and butter, and set the heat to high. Add the cabbage and cook, stirring occasionally, until the liquid in the pan is bubbling and steaming. Reduce the heat to medium, and add the provolone. Toss the pasta with the cheese. The cheese should melt and begin to form a creamy sauce for the pasta. Add the speck, and continue to toss the pasta. When the cheese is fully melted, taste the pasta. Adjust with salt or lemon juice as necessary. Serve it up.

16. Butternut Squash And Gorgonzola Tart

Serving: Serves 6 to 8 | Prep: | Cook: |Ready in:

Ingredients

- Tart Crust
- 2 1/2 cups all purpose flour
- 1/4 cup semolina flour
- 1 teaspoon salt
- 1 teaspoon dried rosemary
- 1 teaspoon dried oregano
- 12 tablespoons unsalted butter, cold
- 1/4-1/2 cups ice water
- For the Filling
- 2 cups roasted butternut squash, mashed
- 1/2 medium onion, diced
- 1/4 teaspoon rosemary salt
- 1/2 teaspoon dried oregano
- 1/2 teaspoon crushed red pepper flakes

- 2 garlic cloves, minced
- 1/2 teaspoon salt
- 1/2 cup whole milk ricotta cheese + additional for serving
- 1/2 cup gorgonzola cheese, crumbled + additional for serving
- 1 egg, beaten
- roasted red pepper, for garnish
- balsamic vinegar

Direction

- In the bowl of a food processor, combine flour, semolina, salt, rosemary and oregano. Pulse to combine. Add cold butter and pulse until coarse crumbs form. Slowly pour the ice water through the tube of the food processor and stop immediately when the dough starts to form a ball. Remove dough from processor and wrap in plastic wrap and refrigerate for one hour.
- After the dough has chilled, roll out half the dough to a size large enough to fill a tart pan. Fit the dough into the tart pan and up the sides. Remove any excess dough. Chill dough in pan for another 30 minutes.
- Preheat the oven to 400 degrees. Line the chilled tart shell with aluminum foil and pie weights. Bake the tart for 25 minutes. Meanwhile make the filling.
- In a large sauté pan, sauté the onions in 2 teaspoons olive oil until tender. Add garlic and sauté for 2 minutes longer. Add the rosemary salt, dried oregano, red pepper flakes and salt. Stir in the squash. After all the ingredients have been incorporated, let cool slightly.
- After the squash filling has cooled slightly, stir in the ricotta, gorgonzola and egg.
- Remove the tart shell from the oven and remove foil and pie weights. Place filling in shell and place on a baking sheet in the oven. Bake for 25-30 minutes.
- Let the tart cool. (It is just as good served room temperature as warm). Slice the tart and serve with ricotta, red pepper strips, gorgonzola and balsamic vinegar drizzled over the top.

17. Butternut Squash And Roasted Garlic Galette

Serving: Serves 4 to 6 | Prep: 24hours30mins | Cook: 1hours0mins | Ready in:

Ingredients

- Pastry
- 3/4 cup all-purpose flour
- 1/4 cup semolina flour
- 1/2 teaspoon kosher salt
- 6 tablespoons chilled unsalted butter, cut into small pieces
- 2 tablespoons ice water, up to 4 tablespoons
- Filling
- 1 butternut squash
- 2 tablespoons olive oil
- 2 teaspoons fresh thyme leaves, chopped
- 1 clove garlic, chopped
- 1 teaspoon kosher salt
- 1/2 teaspoon freshly ground pepper
- 10 cloves, garlic whole and unpeeled
- 1/2 cup fresh ricotta
- 1 cup grated fontina
- 2 tablespoons grated parmesan

Direction

- To make the dough: Put the flour, semolina, and salt in the bowl of a food processor. Pulse to combine. Add the butter and pulse to form a mixture that looks like small peas. Add the ice water, 1 tablespoon at a time, until the dough sticks together (to test, remove the top and gather the dough in your fingers. If it sticks together without crumbling, it's ready). Add the ice water while pulsing, until the dough comes together, being careful not to over mix. Transfer to a lightly floured board and shape the dough into a disk. Wrap tightly in plastic and refrigerate for at least 30 minutes and up to 24 hours.

- Preheat the oven to 400°F. Line 2 baking sheets with parchment paper.
- To make the filling: Cut the squash into two pieces to separate the rounder part from the narrower section. Peel the entire squash, cut both parts in half and remove any seeds. Cut all four pieces into 1/4-inch-thick slices. Put in a large bowl and add the olive oil, chopped garlic and thyme. Toss to coat evenly. Spread out on one of the prepared baking sheets. Set the bowl aside. Sprinkle the squash with the salt and pepper. Put the garlic on the baking sheet and bake until the squash and garlic are tender, about 25-30 minutes. Let cool.
- Remove the dough from the refrigerator and roll out the dough into a large circle about 1/4-inch thick. Transfer to parchment paper–lined baking sheet and refrigerate until ready to use.
- When the garlic is cool enough to handle, peel and put in the reserved bowl. Mash with the back of a wooden spoon until smooth. Stir in the ricotta.
- Remove the pastry from the fridge and spread the garlic-cheese mixture over the top, leaving a 1-inch border. Spread the squash over the garlic-cheese mixture and fold the edges toward the center of the galette. Sprinkle the fontina over the center of the galette. Sprinkle the edges of the crust with the parmesan and bake until the crust is crisp and golden brown, about 25-30 minutes. Let cool slightly before slicing and serving.

18. Butternut Squash Ravioli With Crispy Sage Butter Sauce

Serving: Makes 40 large ravioli | Prep: | Cook: | Ready in:

Ingredients

- Pasta dough and filling
- 14 ounces of 00 pasta flour (about 2 ½ cups)
- 4 eggs
- Semolina flour for dusting surface when you are stretching it
- 1 lb peeled butternut squash, cut up in 1-inch pieces
- Kosher salt
- 2 tablespoons olive oil
- 1 medium onion, peeled and diced small
- 1 garlic clove, peeled and ground to a paste with 1 teaspoon of kosher salt
- 2 Tablespoons real maple syrup
- 1 teaspoon freshly ground pepper
- Sage butter
- 6 ounces, unsalted butter, divided
- 40 small, whole sage leaves, divided
- 2 small wedges of lemon

Direction

- Place the flour and the eggs in a food processor bowl and pulse until the mixture is the texture of grainy sand. On a work surface dusted with flour, turn out the dough and knead it for 4-5 minutes until its skin it soft to the touch, like a baby's skin. Form it into a disk, cover completely with plastic and let it rest in the fridge for at least 30 minutes, but as long as overnight.
- Toss the squash in olive oil and roast them at about 375 degrees until tender. Timing will vary based on how big your have cut your pieces. Once fork tender remove the squash from the oven and cool slightly.
- Place the squash in the tub of a food processor with maple syrup, garlic/salt paste, and freshly ground black pepper. Pulse until you get a creamy puree. Put puree into a medium sized bowl.
- Sauté chopped onions in olive oil until they are soft, but not browned. Stir onions into the puree and cool completely.
- Score the pasta dough disk in eight equal triangles. Working with one piece at a time (cover the remainder with plastic wrap), use a pasta press machine to roll the dough into sheets that have a 1 mm thickness and are about 4 inches wide. Lay the sheet on a lightly floured surface. On the top half of the sheet,

about every 2 inches put a tablespoon puree. Take your finger, dip it in cold water and run your wet finger around each dab of puree. Fold the bottom half of the sheet upwards to cover the dabs of puree. Seal each bubble of puree tightly and cut them apart.
- Place the stuffed ravioli on a sheet tray dusted with semolina or cornmeal and have them dry for about 30 minutes or so.
- While the ravioli cooks, melt butter over medium heat in a large skill. Once the butter is melted, add the sage leaves. The butter will foam and the leaves will crisp up. As soon as the butter starts to turn brown, remove the pan from the heat and squeeze the juice of the lemons into it. Drain the ravioli, turn them into the pan with the sage butter sauce and coat all of them completely.
- Plate the ravioli (I like to sprinkle a little sea salt and freshly ground pepper over them) and serve immediately.

19. Cardamom Cookies Aka Naan Khatai

Serving: Makes 20 to 25 | Prep: | Cook: |Ready in:

Ingredients

- 1 cup All purpose flour
- 2 tablespoons Semolina
- 1 1/2 cups sugar
- 1/2 cup ghee or 1 stick butter
- 2 teaspoons Crushed Cardamom powder
- Pinch Baking Powder
- 2 tablespoons Pistachios sliced
- 2 tablespoons Almond sliced
- 2 teaspoons Rose Water (Optional)
- 1 to 2 teaspoons Warm Milk
- 1 cup Whole-Wheat Flour
- 1 tablespoon Chickpea Flour

Direction

- Add the both the flour (AP flour+ Whole-wheat) and semolina along with chickpea flour, crushed cardamom powder and baking powder. In another bowl, take the ghee and sugar and beat it with a stand mixer until fluffy. Mix the dry mixture to the ghee or butter mixture. Add the rose water also. Add milk to it one teaspoon at a time and as needed. Knead dough. Keep aside this dough for about half an hour hours.
- Preheat the oven to 350 degrees F. Line a cookie sheet greased with butter. Divide the dough into equal parts and roll them into balls with your palms and place them on the baking sheet. With the help of your palms flatten the balls a little bit, press the almond slices and pistachios slices on each cookie. Bake them at 350 degrees F around 20 minutes or until golden brown in color. Once baked, let them cool. Cookies are ready to serve with coffee or tea.

20. Carrot Rava Upma

Serving: Serves 3 | Prep: | Cook: |Ready in:

Ingredients

- 1 cup rava / semolina
- 1 onion, finely chopped
- 1 cup grated carrot
- 2 green chillies, chopped
- A few curry leaves(Optional)
- 1/4 tsp Black mustard seeds
- 2 tsp oil
- Salt to taste

Direction

- Heat oil in pan and add the mustard seeds when mustard seeds splutter add the onion green chili and curry leaves. Fry for few minute then add the carrot stair for few minute

- Now add the semolina into the carrot mix and fry for few minute
- Take all from the pan and keep aside.
- Into the same hot pan add 2 cups of water. When water boils and bubbles add the semolina carrot and mix well.
- Serve hot with lime pickle, sugar or honey.

21. Carrot Kheer

Serving: Serves 4 | Prep: | Cook: | Ready in:

Ingredients

- 1 cup Carrots, grated and tightly packed
- 2 tablespoons Semolina
- 1/4 cup Sugar
- 1/4 cup Condensed milk
- 1/4 cup Dried nuts, chopped
- 1/2 teaspoon Green Cardamom powder
- 2 tablespoons Clarified butter

Direction

- Heat 1 tablespoon clarified butter in a pan add cardamom, pistachios, almonds and raisins until golden. Remove and keep aside.
- Add 1 tablespoon of more clarified butter in the same pan and add carrots and semolina. Cook until carrots are slightly tender for about 4-5 minutes.
- Add condensed milk and whole milk and cook on low flame until carrots are mixed together with milk. Add sugar and cook for 5 minutes more, add fried nuts and serve hot or cold.

22. Cauliflower Fritters

Serving: Serves 4 | Prep: | Cook: | Ready in:

Ingredients

- Cauliflower /gobhi - 250 gms Gram flour /besan - 3/4 cup Corn flour - 3/4 cup Semolina /sooji - 1/4 cup Red chili powder - 1tsp Cumin powder - 1 tsp Turmeric powder- 1/4 tsp Salt - to taste Cooking oil- to deep fry

Direction

- Make medium size florets from cauliflower.
- Boil 2 glasses of water add 1/2 tsp of salt and 1/4 tsp of turmeric powder.
- When it start boiling add cauliflower florets and cook for 1 minute.
- Drain and let it cool down completely.
- In a bowl add gram flour, corn flour, turmeric powder, semolina, salt, chili powder and cumin powder.
- Add water in the mixture and whisk well.
- Make a medium thick batter and rest for 10 minutes.
- Dip the cauliflower florets in the batter and deep fry in hot oil on medium heat.
- Fry till golden in colour.
- Drain on a paper napkin and serve hot.

23. Charlotte Druckman's Cacio E Pepe Shortbread

Serving: Serves 10 to 12 | Prep: | Cook: | Ready in:

Ingredients

- 1/2 cup plus 2 teaspoons finely grated Parmesan cheese, using the small holes of a box grater (divided)
- 1/2 cup plus 2 teaspoons finely grated pecorino Romano cheese, using the small holes of a box grater (divided)
- 2 teaspoons coarsely ground black pepper (divided)
- 1 cup (2 sticks) unsalted butter, at room temperature
- 1/2 cup confectioners' sugar
- 1 1/4 teaspoons kosher salt
- 1 1/2 cups all-purpose flour

- 1/2 cup semolina flour
- 1 tablespoon plus 2 teaspoons extra-virgin olive oil (divided)

Direction

- Heat the oven to 350° F with a 10-inch cast-iron skillet in it.
- In a small bowl, combine 2 teaspoons each of the Parmesan and pecorino and 1 teaspoon of the pepper. Set aside.
- In the bowl of a stand mixer fitted with the paddle, beat the butter on low speed for 1 minute or so, until it's smooth and fluffy, like cake frosting. Add the sugar, salt, and remaining 1 teaspoon pepper and mix until combined. Turn off the mixer and, using a rubber spatula, scrape down the sides of the bowl. Set the speed to medium and mix for 4 to 5 minutes more, until the mixture takes on a thick, creamy, almost shiny texture, like mayonnaise.
- Turn off the mixer and scrape down the sides of the bowl again. Add the all-purpose and semolina flours and mix on low speed to incorporate. Turn off the mixer, scrape down the sides of the bowl one more time, add the remaining 1/2 cup Parmesan and 1/2 cup pecorino, and mix for 1 minute. Using the rubber spatula, push the dough together to form a ball.
- Remove the hot skillet from the oven and brush it with 1 teaspoon of the olive oil. Turn the dough into the skillet and, working quickly, using your fingers (but being careful of the hot pan), press the dough into the skillet, pushing it out to fill the edges and flattening it to create an even surface. Brush with the remaining 1 tablespoon plus 1 teaspoon olive oil. Sprinkle the dough with the cheese-pepper mixture.
- Bake the shortbread for 18 to 23 minutes, until the edges begin to brown. The middle should be cooked through, but slightly soft; it will harden as it cools. Let cool for 10 minutes. Using a plate, carefully invert the pan and flip the shortbread out, then flip it once more onto another plate, so that it's right-side up. Let cool completely. (Or simply cool, slice, and serve from the pan.)
- To serve, divide the shortbread into 10 to 12 wedges. Enjoy it with your afternoon coffee or aperitifs. Like Prosecco, Bellini, rosé, or whatever you like to drink at cocktail hour.

24. Cinnamon Tagliatelle With Stracciatella Di Bufula & Spinach

Serving: Serves 6 | Prep: | Cook: | Ready in:

Ingredients

- Pasta
- 500 grams Type 00 Flour
- 5 Eggs
- 2 teaspoons Ground Cinnamon (Sri Lankan, More Earthy Cinnamon)
- Semolina flour, for rolling and dusting
- Sauce
- 8 ounces Fresh Mascarpone
- 1 packet Stracciatella di Bufula, sliced
- 2 pinches Freshly ground numeg
- 2 pinches Freshly ground black pepper
- 1 pinch salt
- 1 bunch fresh spinach, stems removed and washed
- 1/3 cup Freshly grated parmigiano reggiano (for pasta sauce)
- 1/2 cup Freshly grated parmigiano reggiano (for serving, optional)
- 2 tablespoons fresh cream
- 2 garlic cloves, minced
- 2 tablespoons unsalted butter

Direction

- Take a large wooden cutting board out and place somewhere you have ample room to move around; Place flour on the cutting board and create a well with an opening in the center of the flour. Make sure you put the flour up high enough around the hole- think of a water reservoir. Your hole should be wide, about 4 inches or so in diameter but don't bring out any measurements! This is supposed to be messy; Pour the five eggs in the center of the well; Add the cinnamon to the center and use a fork to beat the eggs slightly and begin to incorporate the flour; Continue to incorporate the flour using your hands until all of the flour and eggs are well mixed together. The dough should be a bit tough to work with but if the dough is too dry, soak your hands in a bit of water to help knead; if it is too soft, add a bit more flour; Continue to knead the dough with your hand for about 10 minutes or so and form a ball; Place in bowl and cover with plastic wrap and leave to rest for an hour in a darker location (not under the light) or in the fridge; When ready to roll out your pasta, dust your cutting board with flour and semolina; Cut your dough depending on the size of your pasta maker- mine is quite small so I cut the dough into an inch thick piece or so (came out to 5 slices);Roll out with rolling pin to make a longer piece with the width of the pasta machine size; Put the sheet through the pasta machine 2-3 times, continuously making the setting smaller. This is how you get the right thickness you are looking for your pasta. I usually end up on setting 4 or 5; Follow with the pasta machine addition to slice into tagliatelle; Place pasta through the pasta machine addition and then place pasta on another cutting board dusted with semolina; and Repeat for remaining dough.

- In a large pot, prepare water for pasta to boil with some sea salt; When water starts to boil, add pasta, stir occasionally and cook for several minutes until it begins to float and is al dente when you taste it; Place pasta in colander and let it sit while you prepare the sauce; Place butter in pot over medium heat and add garlic once melted; Cook garlic for several minutes to add flavor to the butter; Add the spinach and sauté in the garlic butter until almost weltering; Lower heat and add mascarpone in and mix in will with wooden spoon; Add stracciatella di bufala and when it begin to melt well, re add the pasta along with the cream and 1/3 cup of Parmigiano-Reggiano; Mix all together until well combined gently using tongs; Grate nutmeg and black pepper and season with salt; Taste to make sure well spiced and add more cream if the pasta needs it ;and Remove and serve immediately with freshly grated Parmigiano-Reggiano on top.

25. Coconut Quinoa Pudding

Serving: Makes about 6 servings | Prep: | Cook: |Ready in:

Ingredients

- For the quinoa and topping
- 1 cup rinsed and drained quinoa
- 2 cups coconut milk (I used Silk original from the dairy case)
- 1/2 cup grated sweetened coconut
- 1/2 teaspoon cinnamon
- Putting it all together
- 2 cups coconut milk
- 1/3 cup semolina
- 1 tablespoon cornstarch
- A pinch of salt
- 2/3 cup sugar, divided
- 2 large eggs
- 1 cup grated sweetened coconut
- 1 tablespoon grated fresh orange zest
- Juice of one orange
- 2 teaspoons vanilla extract
- Cooked quinoa
- Coconut-cinnamon topping

Direction

- For the quinoa and topping
- In a medium saucepan combine the quinoa and coconut milk. Bring to a boil and then cover and lower the heat to a simmer for about

- 15 minutes until the liquid is absorbed into the grain. Set aside.
- Spread the coconut on a baking sheet and place in a 350° F oven for 5 to 8 minutes, stirring occasionally, until the coconut starts to slightly brown. Place in a small bowl and stir in the cinnamon. Set that bowl aside.
- Putting it all together
- Whisk the semolina, cornstarch, 1/3 cup sugar and the pinch of salt in a small mixing bowl and set aside.
- In a medium saucepan, begin slowly heating the coconut milk to boiling. While watching the milk, beat the eggs with an electric mixer, add the remaining 1/3 cup sugar and continue beating until thick and a little fluffy.
- Once the milk comes up to a boil, whisk in the semolina mixture and continue stirring until the mixture thickens and just starts to boil again. Take off the heat and let rest for about 2 minutes.
- Stir in the egg mixture, cooked quinoa, orange zest, orange juice, coconut, and vanilla. Pour into a greased 8 x 11-inch baking pan. Bake at 350° F for 35 to 40 minutes.
- Serve warm in small dessert dishes topped with a teaspoon or two of the cinnamon-coconut topping.

26. Crispy Moroccan Pancakes (M'smmen)

Serving: Makes 8 pancakes | Prep: 1hours0mins | Cook: 0hours5mins | Ready in:

Ingredients

- 1 1/3 cups semolina flour, divided
- 3 cups all-purpose flour
- 1 tablespoon salt
- 1 1/2 cups warm water
- 1/2 cup melted butter
- 1/2 cup vegetable oil
- 2 tablespoons argan oil, for dipping
- 3 tablespoons honey, for dipping

Direction

- In a large bowl, mix together 2/3 cup semolina, all-purpose flour, and salt. Stir in the warm water, then knead the mixture to obtain a smooth dough. Roll it into a ball and let it rest for 15 minutes.
- Divide the dough into 1 1/2 inches in diameter, and coat each ball with vegetable oil. Let the dough rest for another 15 minutes.
- On an oiled surface, use your hands to flatten out each ball of dough in a thin layer. Brush with melted butter and vegetable oil and sprinkle with the remaining semolina.
- Take one of the balls of dough, and fold one side of the dough 2/3 in across the dough. Then, fold the other side over the overlapping dough. This should make a long strip of 3 layers of thin dough. Fold the two ends of the dough 1/3 of the way in so that they meet in the middle. You should now have a rectangle of dough. Fold it one last time across the middle to make a perfect square approximately 4 inches wide. Repeat with each ball of dough.
- Place a griddle over medium heat, and while it warms up, use your hand to gently flatten the squares into larger, thinner squares, about 6 inches wide.
- Immediately place the flattened dough onto the pan or griddle and cook on each side until golden brown.
- Serve hot off the griddle. Roll the m'smmen, dip it into argan oil, then dip it into honey and enjoy!

27. Crème Fraîche Plum Cake With Plum Caramel

Serving: Makes one 9-inch cake | Prep: | Cook: | Ready in:

Ingredients

- For the plum caramel:
- 3/4 pound ripe plums
- 1 tablespoon freshly squeezed lemon juice
- 1/2 vanilla bean
- 3/4 cup sugar
- For the cake:
- 2 3/4 cups all-purpose flour
- 1 cup sugar, plus 1 tablespoon for sprinkling
- 1/4 cup semolina flour
- 1 1/2 teaspoons baking powder
- 1/2 teaspoon baking soda
- 1/2 teaspoon kosher salt
- 18 tablespoons (2 1/4 sticks) unsalted butter, softened, at room temperature, plus a little for greasing the pan
- 1 cup crème fraîche, divided
- 6 egg yolks
- 3/4 pound ripe plums

Direction

- To make the caramel: Pit the plums and cut them into small wedges. Place them in a blender with the lemon juice and purée until smooth and liquidy. If you are using ripe, juicy plums, you won't need to add any more liquid to make the purée a pourable consistency.
- Use a paring knife to split the vanilla bean in half lengthwise. Scrape the seeds and pulp into a medium saucepan. Add the vanilla bean pod, the sugar, and 1/2 cup water.
- Bring to a boil over medium heat, without stirring. Cook for about 10 minutes, swirling occasionally, until the mixture is a deep amber color. Slowly add the plum purée, whisking constantly. Continue cooking until any sugar that has seized is dissolved. Turn off the heat and let cool. Makes 1 cup plum caramel.
- Preheat the oven to 375° F. Butter a 9-inch round springform pan, line the bottom with parchment paper, and butter the parchment.
- In the bowl of a stand mixer fitted with a paddle attachment, combine the flour, 1 cup sugar, semolina, baking powder, baking soda, and salt. Paddle just to combine.
- Add the butter and 1/2 cup crème fraîche and paddle until the mixture starts to come together but is still crumbly.
- Add the remaining 1/2 cup crème fraîche and the egg yolks, then increase the speed to medium-high and paddle until the color lightens to a pale yellow.
- Remove the pits from the plums and cut them into 3/4-inch wedges.
- Spread half the batter into the prepared pan. Drizzle 1/3 cup plum caramel over the batter, then arrange half the plum wedges on top.
- Dot the remaining half of the batter on top of the arranged plums and caramel, then gently spread it to cover the plums. Arrange the rest of the plum wedges on top, then sprinkle with the final 1 tablespoon sugar.
- Put the cake in the oven with a sheet tray on the rack underneath to capture any caramel drips. Bake for 30 minutes, then reduce the oven temperature to 350° F and bake for 30 more minutes, until the cake begins to pull away from the sides of the pan and a toothpick inserted into the center comes out clean. Cool the cake on a rack for at least 30 minutes before unmolding.
- Serve the cake drizzled with additional plum caramel.

28. Cuban Bread Inspired Sandwich Rolls

Serving: Makes 6 generous sized rolls | Prep: | Cook: | Ready in:

Ingredients

- 1 ¼ cups water
- 2 ½ teaspoons active dry yeast
- ¼ cup fine quality leaf lard (or non-hydrogenated shortening, if good lard is not available)
- 3 ½ cups all purpose flour + more, if necessary, for kneading

- 3/8 cup (1/4 cup + 2 tablespoons) semolina flour
- 2 tablespoons toasted wheat germ
- 1 heaping tablespoon brown sugar
- 1 ½ teaspoon salt
- 1/2 teaspoon olive oil for your bowl during the first rise
- More semolina and Kosher salt, for baking the rolls

Direction

- Heat one cup of the water until it's very hot to the touch. Put it in a large bowl, with the lard, the salt and sugar. Stir it a bit; then set it aside.
- Proof the yeast in ¼ cup of warm water with a tiny pinch of sugar.
- Add one cup of all-purpose flour, the semolina flour and the wheat germ to the bowl with the water and lard. Beat well, all in the same direction.
- Add the proofed yeast and water and two cups of all-purpose flour and stir to combine, as best you can. Turn the contents of the bowl onto a floured work surface and knead until the dough comes together. Gradually add the remaining ½ cup of flour, kneading all the while. (You may not need all the flour. Stop adding it when the dough is still just a bit tacky, and then add only a teaspoon at most more at a time, if absolutely necessary.)
- Rinse and dry your work bowl, then drizzle the olive oil in it and put the kneaded dough, shaped in a neat ball, into the bowl. Cover it with a damp tea towel and let it rise for at least an hour.
- Punch the dough down and remove it to a well-floured work surface (one where you can allow the rolls to rise). Let the dough rest for about five minutes, then cut it into 6 equal pieces. I do this by shaping it first into a square, then using a bench scraper to cut the square down the middle vertically, then dividing each half into three pieces, horizontally.
- Take each rectangle and fold it in thirds, as if you were folding a business letter, bringing the top edge of the longer side and 1/3 of the dough toward you, and then folding the bottom edge up and over that. Press each one down gently with the palm of your hands, doing your best to maintain the rectangular shape.
- Sprinkle them lightly with flour, then cover them with a tea towel and let them rise for 40 - 45 minutes.
- Press down the rectangles of dough until they are somewhat flat. Use the same folding motion with the dough that you used before, then flatten the dough very gently, and fold again. True up the short ends with the sides of your hands to make the rolls as rectangular as you can. If they aren't perfect, don't worry about it.
- Combine about 2 teaspoons of semolina with about 1/2 teaspoon of kosher salt. Sprinkle it on a parchment lined baking sheet; put each roll on it, seam-side up; then turn each seam-side down. Arrange the rolls so there are at least 2 inches between them. Cover with a tea towel and allow them to rise for another thirty minutes.
- Preheat the oven to 375 degrees.
- Bake the rolls for 20 -25 minutes, or until they make a hollow sound when tapped on the bottom. Allow to cool for at least 30 minutes before using.
- Enjoy!!
- N.B. This dough also makes a great loaf. Just shape it and let it rise the second time in the pan in which you are going to bake it. (Or, if you like to use clay pots, as I do, see my "Everyday Potato Bread" recipe for further instructions.) In my really well insulated, reliable convection oven, I bake the loaf at 350 degrees (equivalent of 375 for non-convection ovens, I'm told) for 25 minutes, then tent it lightly with foil and bake for another 25 minutes. It only needs two rises. The second should be about 30 minutes long. You don't want it to double the second time, or the crumb won't be as good for slicing and using for sandwiches.

29. Cumin Pea And Bulgur Fritters With Lemon Yogurt Sauce

Serving: Serves 4-6 | Prep: | Cook: | Ready in:

Ingredients

- Fritters
- 3 cups frozen or fresh green peas
- 1 cup bulgur wheat
- 2 cups water
- 2 teaspoons cumin
- 1/2 teaspoon ground black pepper
- 1/2 teaspoon garlic powder
- salt to taste
- 2 tablespoons semolina
- 6 tablespoons olive oil
- Lemon yogurt sauce
- 1 cup organic non fat natural yogurt
- 4 teaspoons freshly squeezed lemon juice
- 1 lemon for zest
- 2 mild red chili (optional)

Direction

- Cook frozen green peas in a boiling water for a few minutes (until they float) and drain. If you are using fresh peas, simply wash them and drain. Puree them in a food processor and set aside to cool. Boil 2 cups of water in a pot and add bulgur wheat. Stir for 1 minute, bring the heat down to low and cover to simmer gently for 14-15 minutes. When bulgur wheat is cooked and all the water has been absorbed, remove from the heat and mix with pea puree in a bowl. Leave it to cool for a few minutes.
- Season the mixture with cumin, ground black pepper and garlic powder. Taste and add a little pinch of salt to your liking. Stir in semolina to bind everything together. Shape the mixture into a 4-5cm diameter and 1.5cm thick round patties. You should have minimum of 24 patties in total. Place them in a fridge to set for 45 minutes to 1 hour. Meanwhile, prepare lemon yogurt sauce and set aside. Finely chop and deseed red chili then set aside separately.
- Add olive oil in a medium heat non-stick pan. Gently place the patties (add a little more oil if necessary), making sure they don't burn. I divided my patties into 3 batches, so used 2 tablespoons of oil per batch. It should take about 2-3 minutes on each side to cook to golden and crispy. When they are ready remove from the heat, place onto paper towel and gently pat down.
- After cooling the fritters for a few minutes plate them with lemon yogurt sauce and red chili garnish.

30. Cumin Orange Chocolate Semolina Pudding

Serving: Serves 6 | Prep: | Cook: | Ready in:

Ingredients

- 4 cups whole milk (divided)
- 6 tablespoons semolina
- 2 tablespoons butter
- 4 ounces dark chocolate
- 2 tablespoons agave nectar (or honey)
- 1 teaspoon orange zest
- 1/2 teaspoon cumin

Direction

- Fill a large skillet with water, and heat to just below simmering. Place the chocolate and one cup of milk in a heatproof bowl (stainless steel, glass, etc.) and place the bowl in the water. Gently and constantly stir till the chocolate is completely melted. Stir in cumin and orange zest. Remove from the heat and set a side
- Put 3 cups of milk and agave nectar in a heavy bottom pan over medium heat. Sprinkle the semolina slowly, and stir constantly till it starts to boil and thicken. Add the chocolate mixture, and stir until completely mixed.

- Finally, stir in the butter and remove from the heat.
- Divide between 6 serving bowls. Cool slightly, and serve warm. Alternatively, cool completely and refrigerate for a couple of hours. The pudding will thicken even more in the fridge, and will be easily removed from the bowls. Turn them upside down on individual plates, and sprinkle with some more orange zest before serving.

31. Custard Filled Mini Phyllo Cups

Serving: Makes about 60 | Prep: 0hours0mins | Cook: 0hours0mins | Ready in:

Ingredients

- 2 cups whole milk
- 1/3 cup semolina, farina or Cream of Wheat
- 1 tablespoon cornstarch
- A pinch of salt
- 2/3 cup sugar, divided
- 2 large eggs
- 1 tablespoon fresh orange zest
- 1 teaspoon vanilla extract
- 1 tablespoon honey
- 4 packages mini phyllo (fillo) shells (15 per pack)
- 1/2 to 3/4 cups walnuts toasted in a 350F oven for 5 minutes and then chopped
- Honey for drizzling

Direction

- Whisk the semolina, cornstarch, 1/3 cup of the sugar and the pinch of salt in a small mixing bowl and set aside
- In a medium sauce pan begin slowly heating the milk to boiling. While watching the milk, beat the eggs with an electric mixer, add the remaining 1/3 cup sugar and continue beating until fluffy.
- Once the milk comes up to the boil, whisk in the semolina mixture and continue stirring until the mixture thickens and just starts to boil again. Take off the heat and let rest for about 2 minutes.
- Stir in the egg/sugar mixture, vanilla, honey and orange zest.
- Place the mini phyllo cups on baking sheets and fill each with the custard, almost to the top. Bake in a 350F oven for 6 to 8 minutes until the custard is set.
- Remove from the oven, sprinkle with the walnuts and then drizzle each cup with a few drops of honey.

32. Deconstructed Pesto With A Saute Of Sausage, Peppers, And Onions

Serving: Serves six | Prep: | Cook: | Ready in:

Ingredients

- Basil Pasta (makes one pound)
- 1 1/2 tablespoons olive oil
- 1/3 cup packed, fresh basil leaves
- 1 cake semolina flour
- 1 cup all purpose flour
- 1/2 teaspoon salt
- 3 eggs; at room temperature
- Deconstructed Pesto with a Saute of Sausage, Peppers, and Onions
- Basil pasta
- 1 tablespoon butter
- 1 cup heavy cream
- 1/2 cup half and half
- 8 cloves of garlic; roasted and then mashed in a bowl with a fork
- 1 egg yolk; slightly beaten
- 4 ounces parmesan cheese; grated. Plus more for topping
- 1 tablespoon olive oil
- 1 yellow onion; sliced thin
- 1 red pepper; sliced thin
- 4 sweet Italian sausage links; sliced into 3/4 inch pieces

- 1/2 cup pine nuts; toasted. For topping

Direction

- Basil Pasta (makes one pound)
- In the bowl of a food processor puree the basil leaves and the olive oil. Set aside.
- In a medium sized bowl combine the semolina flour, all-purpose flour, and salt. Mix until well incorporated. Make a well in the center of the flours. Crack the eggs into the well and add in the basil puree. Using a fork, blend the ingredients in the well, slowly drawing in the flour until everything is combined into a dough.
- Dust a clean work surface with flour and transfer the dough to that surface. Knead the dough until it feels smooth, about 8- 10 minutes.
- Wrap the dough in plastic wrap and allow it to rest at room temperature for 1/2 an hour.
- Using either a pasta machine or a rolling pin roll out your pasta and cut it into fettuccini width noodles.
- At this point the pasta can be used or frozen for later use.
- Deconstructed Pesto with a Sauté of Sausage, Peppers, and Onions
- Set a large pot of salted water over high heat and bring it to a rolling boil.
- Meanwhile, in a medium saucepan over medium heat melt the butter. Add the heavy cream, the half and half, and whisk in the roasted garlic. Bring to a boil, reduce the heat to low and simmer until the cream is reduced by 1/4, about 10 minutes.
- Stir a generous spoonful of the cream into a bowl with the egg yolk, then return the mixture to the saucepan with the rest of the cream, mixing well. Add in the parmesan cheese. Season with salt and pepper to taste. Set on a back burner with a lid on to keep warm.
- In a large sauté pan over medium heat warm the olive oil. Once the olive oil is heated add in the sweet Italian sausage. Once the sausage is cooked through, about 5 minutes. Remove the sausage from pan with a slotted spoon, to a plate and set aside. In the same sauté pan now add the pepper and onion. Sauté until softened, about 10 minutes. Put the sausage back in the pan and mix it into the pepper and onion.
- While the pepper and onion are sautéing cook the basil pasta. Remember that since you are using fresh pasta it will only take a couple of minutes for the pasta to cook.
- Drain pasta and place it in a serving bowl. Mix half of the roasted garlic cream sauce into the pasta then pour the remaining half over the pasta. Top with the sausage, pepper, and onion sauté. Finish with a sprinkling of parmesan and pine nuts. Serve immediately.

33. Deep Dish Pizza Dough

Serving: Makes 2 pounds | Prep: 1hours10mins | Cook: 0hours0mins | Ready in:

Ingredients

- 4 cups (482 grams) all-purpose flour
- 1/3 cup (54 grams) semolina flour
- 1 1/2 teaspoons (6 grams) fine sea salt
- 1 tablespoon (9 grams) instant active dry yeast
- 1/3 cup (81 grams) extra-virgin olive oil
- 1 1/2 cups (363 grams) warm water

Direction

- In the bowl of an electric mixer fitted with the dough hook attachment, mix the all-purpose flour, semolina flour, salt, and yeast to combine.
- Add the olive oil and water and mix on low speed for 2 minutes. Raise speed to medium and mix for 3 minutes more.
- Transfer the dough to a large oiled bowl and cover with plastic wrap. Let rise until double in size, about 45 minutes-1 hour. At this point, the dough can be used or wrapped tightly and

refrigerated for up to 3 days. Bring to room temperature before using.

34. English Muffins

Serving: Makes about 15 muffins | Prep: 0hours0mins | Cook: 0hours0mins | Ready in:

Ingredients

- 5 1/2 cups (27 ounces) bread flour
- 1 tablespoon (0.35 ounces) instant dry yeast
- 1 1/2 tablespoons (0.75 ounces) salt
- 2 teaspoons (0.25 ounces) sugar
- 2 1/4 cups (19.25 ounces) room temperature water
- 4 tablespoons (2 ounces) room temperature butter
- 1 pinch semolina flour, for dipping

Direction

- Make the dough the day before you want to make the English muffins. To make the dough, combine the bread flour, yeast, salt, and sugar in the bowl of an electric mixer fitted with the dough hook. Mix on low speed for 20 to 30 seconds, just to combine.
- Add the water and the butter and mix on low speed for 4 minutes. Scrape down the sides of the bowl and scrape the dough away from the hook. Raise the speed to medium and mix for 3 minutes more. The dough should be smooth—if it feels tacky or sticky, add more flour, 1 tablespoon at a time, until it's smooth and easy to handle.
- Transfer the dough to a large, oiled bowl and cover with plastic wrap. Transfer the dough to the refrigerator and let rise overnight.
- Bring the dough to room temperature before proceeding (20 to 30 minutes).
- On a lightly floured surface, roll out the dough to 1/2-inch thick. Using a bench knife or a pastry wheel, cut the dough into squares that are 2 1/2 by 2 1/2 inches.
- Cover the shaped muffins and let rise for 15 to 20 minutes on your work surface. After the muffins have risen, dip each one in semolina flour on both sides.
- Preheat the oven to 475° F. Line two baking sheets with parchment paper.
- Heat a large cast-iron skillet (or griddle) over medium-high heat. When the skillet is nice and hot, add the shaped muffins (as many as you can without crowding—you should be able to easily turn them over). Cook until golden brown, 2 to 4 minutes. Flip the muffin and cook until golden on the other side, another 2 to 4 minutes.
- Transfer the muffins to the prepared baking sheets, and bake until a thermometer inserted into the center reads somewhere between 200 and 215° F, 8-10 minutes. The muffins won't brown much more, but the interior will bake through.
- Cool 5 to 10 minutes before serving. If you've made the muffins ahead, cool completely and store in an airtight container. Reheat in a low temperature oven or in the toaster before serving.

35. Fire Roasted Red Pepper Semolina Soup

Serving: Serves 4-6 | Prep: | Cook: | Ready in:

Ingredients

- 3-4 cups broth made from red peppers, herbs, tomatoes, carrot, and onion
- bouquet garni of thyme, parsley, basil, sage or similar herbs
- 1 cardamom pod
- 2 teaspoons pink or kosher salt, to taste
- 1/2-3/4 cups pureed red peppers (and you could include some tomato carrot and onion, too, in this mix, if desired)
- 1 tablespoon sweet or smoked paprika (Hungarian preferred)

- 2 teaspoons ground cumin
- 1 tablespoon clarified butter/ghee, or high grade unsalted regular butter
- 1/2 cup semolina
- 3 tablespoons EVOO
- 1/2 cup milk
- 1 egg
- splash of white wine, optional
- splash of vodka, optional
- 2-3 fire roasted peppers, cut into slivers
- 2 tablespoons Korean bell pepper threads, shilgochu, optional
- fresh herbs or capers for garnish, optional
- sprinkle of paprika for garnish
- additional EVOO for drizzle

Direction

- Start by making a 4 pints of great vegetable broth which includes filtered water, at least 2 sweet de-seeded red peppers, at least 1 tomato, 1 carrot, 1 onion, and the salt. Add a bouquet garni of thyme, sage, basil, and parsley to the broth. I use plain dental floss to tie the herbs together, but string works well. Add a cardamom pod, too. You can use all your saved vegetable ends to make this broth. Do include one fire roasted pepper into this broth as well as one uncooked sweet red pepper for depth of flavor. Give the broth at least an hour to simmer. Strain the broth and save any good pepper bits from which you can make your puree. Have about 4 cups of strained great broth in the end. From this, salvage about 1/2-3/4 cup of cooked red pepper (and a few other choice vegetables with a bit of tomato, carrot and onion) and puree. You can add a few tablespoons of broth into the mix to facilitate the puree if helpful. I used a blender.
- Heat ghee (if you have it) or unsalted high grade butter in a large sauté pan; add the paprika and cumin stirring constantly. Next add 3 tbl. of oil and heat for one minute. Add the semolina, stirring constantly for a few minutes. Add the pepper puree mixture into the semolina and continue stirring for a few minutes.
- Next add 3-4 cups of strained broth and simmer over low heat for about 10 minutes. If you are really pressed for time, you can select the best quality vegetable (or even chicken) broth you can find.
- Beat the egg with the milk. Take 1 or 2 tbsps. of the simmering soup from the pot and add it to this mixture to temper. Then add this tempered mix to the soup, whisk in, and continue to simmer for another 5 minutes or so. Add wine and or vodka at this point if desired in the final cooking minutes. If you have stirred continuously this soup should be very smooth. However, if you find a few clumps of the semolina along the way, they just add a bit more texture, not to worry.
- To serve this soup, ladle into the dishes. Arrange a cut fire roasted pepper on top with bell pepper threads, if you like. Drizzle EVOO on top. Garnish with fresh herb or capers and paprika. You can enjoy this soup warm or even cool. Serve with artisan bread! I really hope you make this and enjoy it.

36. Fresh Orecciette With Broccoli Rabe, Sausage And Yellow Raisins

Serving: Serves 4 | Prep: | Cook: | Ready in:

Ingredients

- Orecciette (Little Ears) Pasta
- 1/2 cup warm water
- 1 teaspoon salt
- 1 1/4 cups semolina flour
- AP Flour for dusting
- For the "Sauce"
- 2 tablespoons olive oil
- 1 shallot, minced
- 1 clove garlic, minced
- 1 teaspoon red pepper flakes

- 1 handful yellow raisins
- 1 pound bulk Italian sweet sausage
- 1 bunch broccoli rabe
- 2 sprigs fresh thyme
- 1/2 cup grated Parmigiano-Reggiano cheese
- Salt and pepper to taste

Direction

- Orecchiette (Little Ears) Pasta
- Add salt to warm water.
- In a steady stream, add semolina to salted water, while stirring with a fork.
- When a loose ball forms, turn out onto a floured countertop and knead until satiny and smooth, about 8 minutes.
- Rest dough for 20 minutes under the overturned bowl.
- After 20 minutes, remove dough from bowl and cut into 4 pieces. Place three pieces back under bowl, and roll one into a long thin rope.
- On a floured tea towel (not terry cloth), cut rope into 1/2 inch pieces. Using your thumb, gently press each piece into a round "little ear" shape. Remove to another floured tea towel, rest in a single layer.
- Repeat with remaining pieces of dough. Make sure formed pasta is resting in a single layer. Let dry about 30 minutes while you make the sauce.
- For the "Sauce"
- While pasta is drying, bring a large pot well salted water to a boil.
- Trim ends of broccoli rabe by about 1/2 an inch. Submerge into boiling water, blanch about 2 minutes. Drain, rinse rabe immediately with cold water to stop cooking.
- Refill same pot with water, salt well, bring to boil.
- While waiting for water to boil, add olive oil to a large sauté pan over medium heat. Add shallots, cook about 1 minute. Add garlic, raisins and red pepper flakes, cook about 30 seconds more.
- Add sausage to sauté pan, cook through.
- Finally, add blanched broccoli rabe. Season with salt and pepper.
- When water is boiling, add pasta. Stir briefly. When all pasta has risen to the surface of the water, drain, saving 2 tbsp of pasta water.
- Add pasta to sausage mixture, along with pasta water. Cook about 1 minute more until heated through.
- Toss in cheese along with another drizzle of olive oil. Check for seasoning and serve immediately.

37. Fried Pickled Celery

Serving: Serves 6 to 8 | Prep: | Cook: | Ready in:

Ingredients

- For Quick-Pickled Celery
- 1 bunch celery hearts (about 6 or 8 stalks), root-end trimmed, stalks separated and cut on the bias into 2" lengths (leaves reserved for garnish)
- 1 tsp peppercorns (divided)
- 3 bay leaves (divided)
- Kosher salt, to taste
- 1 cup white vinegar or cider vinegar
- 1/2 cup water
- 3 T sugar
- ¼ tsp celery seeds
- ¼ tsp crushed red chili flakes
- Zest and juice of 1 large lemon
- For Breading, Frying, and Serving
- Peanut or vegetable oil, amount dependent upon the size of your pot or fryer
- 1 cup buttermilk
- 2 cups of all-purpose flour
- ½ cup of semolina flour
- 1/2 tsp of cayenne pepper
- 1 or 2 large lemons, very thinly sliced (as thin as possible!) and seeds removed (optional)
- kosher salt, to taste
- celery leaves, finely chopped

Direction

- For Quick-Pickled Celery

- Put celery into a medium-sized saucepan; cover with water. Add 1/2 tsp peppercorns and 2 bay leaves and season generously with kosher salt. Cover and bring to a boil; reduce heat to medium-low and simmer until celery is tender but not soft, about 10 to 15 minutes. Using tongs, transfer celery to a heat-proof bowl.
- Meanwhile, make the brine by combining vinegar and water in a saucepan with remaining 1/2 tsp peppercorns, 1 bay leaf, sugar, celery seeds, chili flakes, and lemon juice and zest; bring to a boil and then remove from heat. (Brine can be made several days in advance and chilled until ready to use.)
- Pour the brine over the celery and let stand until cool, about 20 to 25 minutes. (If your brine is already chilled, you can skip this cooling step.) Cover the bowl with plastic wrap and refrigerate for at least 1 hour and up to a couple of days.
- For Breading, Frying, and Serving
- In a large pot or fryer, heat oil to 365 to 370 degrees F. You want the oil to be at least a few inches deep, with at least two to three inches of clearance from the top of the pan. While you bread the celery and lemon (if using), closely monitor your oil, adjusting the heat as needed to reach this temperature.
- While the oil is coming to temperature, set up your breading station. Place the buttermilk in a wide, shallow bowl or pie plate. Right next to this bowl, mix the flour, semolina, and cayenne in a wide, shallow bowl or pie plate. Then place a large sheet pan right next to the flour mixture. Place a few pieces of celery in the buttermilk – then transfer them to the bed of flour. Coat all sides. Lift out, tapping or shaking off the excess flour, and transfer them to a sheet pan in a single layer. Repeat with the remaining celery and lemon slices, if using. You can hold the breaded celery and lemons at room temperature for up to ½ hour before frying.
- When the oil is at temperature, fry the celery in small batches. You don't want an overcrowded pot as that leads to a soggy fry.

Using tongs or a fork, very gently turn the celery a few times until it's a deep golden brown on all sides, about 2 minutes. Once done, lift out the celery with tongs or a skimmer, then transfer to a paper-lined plate. Repeat the frying and draining of the remaining celery and lemons (if using) in the same manner, making sure to spread (not stack) the fried food in a single layer to cool.
- Serve hot with a sprinkling of coarse salt and finely chopped celery leaves.

38. Fried Anchovies With Curry Leaves

Serving: Serves 2-3 | Prep: 0hours0mins | Cook: 0hours0mins | Ready in:

Ingredients

- 250 grams anchovies, gutted and cleaned
- 2 cloves of garlic, minced
- 1/4 teaspoon minced ginger
- 1/2 teaspoon chilli powder
- 1/8 teaspoon turmeric powder
- 1 1/2 tablespoons semolina
- 1 tablespoon rice flour
- 10 sprigs curry leaves
- Coconut oil, for deep-frying
- Salt, to taste
- Lemon wedges

Direction

- Add minced garlic, minced ginger, chilli powder, turmeric powder, and salt to a large bowl and mix to a thick paste. Fingers are best for this job. Tip in the anchovies and toss to coat all the pieces evenly. Leave to marinate for at least two hours (or overnight for best results). If you are short on time, it can be used right away.
- Heat coconut oil over medium heat. Mix semolina and corn flour together on a plate and set aside.

- Take a few pieces of the fish and dredge them in the semolina-corn flour mixture before dropping them into the oil. Make sure not to overcrowd the pan. Fry the anchovies for 1-2 minutes until golden and transfer to a paper towel. Repeat in batches.
- Once the anchovies are all fried, drop the sprigs of curry leaves into the oil until they crisp up. Make sure to stand back for this step as the curry leaves will pop and sputter. Drain on paper towels.
- To serve, I like to scrunch up some of the crispy curry leaves in my hand and use as a garnish for the anchovies. Serve with lemon wedges.

39. Frito Pie

Serving: Serves 4 | Prep: | Cook: | Ready in:

Ingredients

- 2 dried ancho chiles, stem and seeds removed
- 2 dried guajillo chiles, stem and seeds removed
- 1 cup hot water
- 1 teaspoon whole coriander seed
- 1 teaspoon whole cumin seed
- 1 teaspoon chile powder
- 1 teaspoon cocoa powder
- 2 tablespoons rendered beef fat (or bacon drippings, or veg oil)
- 1 pound beef chuck roast, diced into 1/2 inch cubes
- 1/2 large white onion, diced
- 2 cloves garlic, minced
- 1 12 oz bottle of beer (I used Shiner Bock)
- 1/2 cinnamon stick
- 1 tablespoon semolina
- kosher salt, to taste
- 4 small bags Fritos
- 3 ounces cheddar cheese, shredded
- 1/2 white onion, minced
- 1/2 cup sour cream, for dolloping

Direction

- Tear the chiles into smaller pieces and toast in a medium-sized Dutch oven set over medium heat for 1-2 minutes. Transfer toasted chiles to a blender, cover with 1 cup of very hot tap water, and allow to sit for 10 minutes. Blend the chiles and water until smooth.
- Toast the cumin and coriander seeds in the now empty pot for a minute or two, until fragrant, and then grind in a mortar and pestle until finely ground. Add the chile powder, cocoa powder, and kosher salt and stir to combine.
- Add the beef fat (or bacon fat, or oil) to the Dutch oven, set over medium heat. Brown the diced beef in two batches, and then remove to sit on a plate.
- Add the onions to the pot and cook for 5 minutes, until soft and caramelized, being sure to scrape up the beef bits on the bottom of the pot. Add the minced garlic and spice blend, and cook for 30 more seconds. Add the browned beef and any accumulated juices, the chile puree, the cinnamon stick, and the bottle of beer. Bring to a boil and then turn the heat to low and simmer for 3 hours.
- Stir in the semolina and season the chili to taste with kosher salt.
- To assemble the Frito Pies, cut open the front of the bags of Fritos, and top each with a few spoonfuls of chili, shredded cheddar cheese, minced onion, and a dollop of sour cream. I hope you like it!

40. Gingerbread Kransecake

Serving: Makes enough to serve a crowd (15-20 people) or just be a lovely centerpiece | Prep: 0hours0mins | Cook: 0hours0mins | Ready in:

Ingredients

- 6 2/3 cups (638 g) almond flour
- 3 cups (340 g) powdered sugar

- 1 tablespoon ground ginger
- 2 teaspoons ground cinnamon
- 1 teaspoon ground cloves
- 1/2 teaspoon ground allspice
- 1/2 teaspoon ground nutmeg
- 5 large (175 g) egg whites
- 1 teaspoon vanilla extract
- 3/4 teaspoon almond extract
- nonstick spray, as needed for prepping molds
- semolina flour or cornmeal, as needed for prepping molds
- 1 recipe Royal Icing (https://food52.com/recipes...)
- silver nonpareils, for decorating (optional)

Direction

- In a large bowl, sift together the almond flour, powdered sugar, ginger, cinnamon, cloves, allspice, and nutmeg to combine. Transfer to the bowl of an electric mixer fitted with the paddle attachment.
- Add the egg whites, vanilla, and almond extract and mix on low speed until the mixture is uniformly combined, 2-3 minutes.
- Wrap the dough tightly in plastic wrap, and refrigerate for 1 1/2 - 2 hours.
- To prepare the molds, lightly grease them with nonstick spray and dust lightly with semolina or cornmeal (be sure to use cornmeal if you want it to be gluten-free).
- When the dough has chilled well, preheat the oven to 400° F.
- Divide the dough into 6 even pieces. Divide each piece into three pieces, but not evenly; you'll want to get one small, one medium, and one larger piece from each. Don't worry about making it perfect. You can always "borrow" extra from other pieces later.
- Take each piece of dough and roll it out on a clean work surface into a rope about 1/2-inch to 3/4-inch thick. You shouldn't need flour, but if the dough is sticking, dust your surface lightly with semolina or cornmeal.
- Place each rope into the prepared mold, following the circle indentations in the mold. Press the dough together firmly where the ends meet to seal. If there's too much dough, pinch it off and save it to add to another piece if needed. Use the larger ropes for the outer rings on each mold, the medium rope for the middle ring, and the smallest rope for the center.
- Repeat until all the dough is used and all the molds are lined. Transfer the molds to the oven (you can place a few together on a baking sheet if you like), and bake until the cookies are lightly golden and feel set, 10-12 minutes.
- Let the cookies cool completely in their molds. When they are cool, carefully remove them (it should be very easy).
- To assemble the kransekake, place royal icing in a pastry bag with a small circle tip. Pipe a few dots onto a serving platter and place the largest ring on top to adhere it to the platter.
- Pipe dots all around the surface of the ring, and place the next largest ring on top. Continue to place dots and rings, working your way up to the smallest ring.
- Decorate the kransekake with the remaining royal icing however you like. I like to do a different design/pattern on every ring, but you can also just do simple lines all the way down or on every other piece.
- Serve immediately or hold for up to 3 days. The cookies are quite crisp and won't "stale" much, so this makes for a great make-ahead that can be stored at room temperature, much like gingerbread used for houses.

41. Gnudi

Serving: Serves 4 to 6 | Prep: | Cook: | Ready in:

Ingredients

- 2 cups whole milk ricotta cheese
- 4 tablespoons freshly grated Parmesan cheese
- 2 tablespoons freshy parsley, finely chopped
- 2 eggs
- 1 pinch freshly grated nutmeg

- sea salt and ground pepper to taste
- 1/2-3/4 cups semolina flour
- 2 cups your favorite marinara sauce

Direction

- In a medium bowl whisk together first six ingredients. Slowly add semolina using just enough to bind everything together, although it will still be a bit loose.
- Chill mixture for 1 hour. Using two spoons (I used deep teaspoons) scoop up the filling and roll it from one spoon to another until you get a perfect, somewhat elongated egg shape. Carefully transfer to a baking sheet dusted with flour. Cover and chill for another hour.
- In a large pot bring 3 quarts of salted water to a rapid boil. Carefully drop half the gnudi into water and lower heat to a gentle boil. Cook for 5 or 6 minutes. Pull out gundi with a ladle or spider and drain. Repeat with the rest of the gnudi. Serve with your favorite marinara sauce.

42. Grilled Flank Steak Piadina With Cannellini Bean Puree And Arugula

Serving: Serves 4 | Prep: | Cook: | Ready in:

Ingredients

- Steak and Marinade
- 1 1/2 pounds flank steak
- 1/4 cup olive oil
- 1/4 cup balsamic vinegar
- 1 tablespoon Worcestershire sauce
- 1 tablespoon soy sauce
- 2 garlic cloves, crushed
- 1 teaspoon onion powder
- 1 teaspoon freshly ground black pepper
- 2 sprigs • Fresh parsley and rosemary to taste
- For the salad, puree, and piadina dough
- 3 1/2 cups whole wheat flour
- 1/2 teaspoon baking soda
- Sea Salt
- 1/2 cup butter, cut into ½ inch cubes, at room temperature
- 3/4 cup water (approx.)
- 1 cup olive oil
- ground semolina for dusting
- 3 garlic cloves, minced
- 1/4 teaspoon crushed red pepper
- 2 cups cooked cannellini beans
- 4 sage leaves
- 2 lemons
- zest of one lemon
- 1 yellow squash, cut into 1/2 in. coins and roasted for 25 minutes at 375 degrees
- 1-2 bunches arugula
- 1/4 cup red onion, sliced paper thin (use a vegetable peeler if necessary!)
- 1/2 teaspoon mustard

Direction

- Combine all ingredients for the steak marinade with your flank steak and place in a freezer bag removing as much air as possible. Lay your freezer bag into a baking dish and refrigerate. Steak can marinate for a minimum of 2 hours, but preferably overnight. Remove the meat from the refrigerator approx. 30 minutes before grilling.
- For the piadina, mix flour, baking soda and 1 tsp. salt in the bowl of a stand mixer, or hand mixer, using the dough hook attachment.
- Add the butter and combine with the mixer. With the machine running, slowly add the water until the dough forms.
- Remove the dough from the mixer and knead for 8-10 minutes, or until smooth. Let the dough rest for 30 minutes in the refrigerator.
- Steps 1-4 can be done in advance
- While your meat is marinating and dough is resting, prepare the bean puree and arugula salad. For the bean puree, drain and rinse the cannellini beans and set aside (or cook beans fully if using dried).
- In a small sauce pan heat 3/4 c. olive oil, and add minced garlic, sage, and crushed red

pepper over medium low heat for 15 minutes and set aside.
- Combine beans, 2 tbsp. lemon juice, lemon zest, and yellow squash in a food processor. Pulse to begin the puree. Slowly add the prepared olive oil mixture.
- Season with salt and pepper and reserve the bean puree
- In a small bowl, combine ¼ c. lemon juice, ½ tsp. mustard, salt and pepper. Slowly whisk in ¼ c. extra-virgin olive oil and dress the arugula and red onion.
- Prepare your grill or grill pan.
- Divide your dough into 4 portions. Roll each portion out to ¼ inch thickness. Brush both sides with olive oil and sprinkle with salt, pepper, and the underside with semolina.
- Grill the piadini and flank steak for 4-5 minutes per side. Grill the steak directly over a high flame to ensure caramelization.
- Allow your steak to rest for 15 minutes. In the meantime, spread bean puree over each of the piadini.
- Thinly slide the steak against the grain on a bias. This slicing method is important to preserve the tender texture of the meat.
- Final Assembly: Place a layer of the dressed arugula over the bean puree and top with a layer of flank steak. Finish with a drizzle of extra-virgin olive oil (one of finishing quality) and light sprinkling of sea salt.

43. Gujia Sweet Empanada

Serving: Makes 6 to 8 | Prep: | Cook: | Ready in:

Ingredients

- For the Pastry shell
- 1 cup of All purpose Flour
- 5 to 6 tbsp of Ghee or Brown butter
- pinch of baking soda
- pinch of salt
- 1 tbsp of confectioner's sugar
- 1 tsp of vanilla bean paste or vanilla essence
- Sweet Coconut Filling
- 1 cup of Freshly grated coconut
- 1/4 cup or more Sugar You can add more or less sugar as per your taste
- 1/2 cup chopped nuts - a mix of cashews, almonds and also raisins
- 1 tbsp of Ghee
- 1 tsp of cardamom powder, optional
- pinch of saffron dissolved in warm milk
- 3 to 4 tbsp semolina
- 1/2 cup of Khoya available at Indian grocery stores in frozen section

Direction

- For the pastry - Mix all the ingredients and make a pastry dough. Cover it and let it sit till we prepare the filling.
- For the filling - Take ghee in a pan, add the nuts and raisins and cook them just for about 2 to 3 seconds, do not let them burn. Immediately add the semolina and cook it for few more seconds, and add all the other ingredients. Cook it till everything is well mixed. Once it is done, remove it and let it cool for a bit before filling them into the pastry shells.
- Divide the dough into equal parts and roll out about 3 to 4 inch diameter, place the filling in the center and fold the dough into the shape of empanada. Seal the edges with your fingers or a fork.
- In another, wok heat some oil for frying these. You can also bake them at 350 F for about 20 to 30 minutes or till perfectly done.

44. Hand Pulled Breadsticks (Grissini Stirati)

Serving: Makes about 25 breadsticks | Prep: | Cook: | Ready in:

Ingredients

- 1 3/4 teaspoons active dry yeast (12 grams fresh yeast)
- 1/2 tablespoon malt syrup or sugar
- 1 1/4 cups (310 ml) lukewarm water
- 2 tablespoons olive oil, plus extra for brushing
- 3 3/4 cups (500 grams) bread flour
- 1 1/2 teaspoons teaspoons salt
- 1/2 cup (85 grams) semolina, for dusting and rolling

Direction

- In a large bowl, combine the yeast, malt syrup, and water. Let sit for about 10 minutes, until the yeast dissolves and becomes foamy. Stir in the olive oil, then add the flour and combine until it comes together into a dough. Knead on a lightly floured surface until smooth, soft, and elastic, about 8 to 10 minutes if doing this by hand (3 minutes if in a mixer). Add in the salt towards the end.
- Using a rolling pin, flatten the dough into a rectangle about 14 inches (35 centimeters) long, then fold into thirds for a width of about 3 to 4 inches (8 to 10 centimeters). Place, seam down, on a well-floured surface. Lightly brush or spray the top with olive oil, loosely cover with plastic wrap, and let rise (in a warm spot, if possible) until doubled, about 1 hour.
- Heat the oven to 450° F (230° C) and lightly oil a baking sheet. To shape the grissini, with a sharp knife, cut the loaf crosswise into pieces that are 3 to 4 inches long and about the width of a finger (a bit more than 1/3 inch or about 1 centimeter wide). Place the semolina on a plate or wide, shallow bowl and roll the dough gently in the semolina to lightly coat. Without disturbing the side of the dough that has just been cut, using your thumbs and forefingers, gently pull the piece of dough from both ends. Stretch to the width or length of your baking sheet. Place on the prepared baking sheet and continue with the rest of the dough.
- Bake until the breadsticks are golden, about 11 to 15 minutes, depending on how thick or thin your breadsticks are. Remove from the oven and cool on baking racks.

45. Homemade Farfalle

Serving: Serves 4 | Prep: | Cook: |Ready in:

Ingredients

- 2 large eggs
- 2/3 cup all-purpose flour
- 2/3 cup semolina flour

Direction

- Mix the all-purpose flour and semolina flour together, then make a volcano-like mound of flour on your work surface. Crack the eggs into the hollow and sprinkle with salt. Then, using a fork, gently stir the eggs, incorporating the flour from the walls of the volcano little by little. Once the dough has become workable by hand -- a fair amount of flour will have been worked in -- use your hands to incorporate the rest of the loose flour. When the dough has come together smoothly, knead the ball for about 5 minutes. If it's feeling moist, incorporate some more flour into the dough. You want to end up with a ball that's not sticky, but still soft. Cover the ball of dough and let it relax for about 30 minutes.
- Cut the dough into four pieces. Keeping the unworked dough covered, take a piece and begin rolling it out with a rolling pin, keeping its shape roughly rectangular. You want it to end up thin, about 1 millimeter in width. Using a sharp knife, slice the pasta into pieces that are about 1 1/2 x 1 inch. Along the long side, pinch each rectangle in the middle very hard. Congrats, you just made pasta! Place the farfalle on a baking sheet liberally dusted with flour and keep it covered. Continue in the same fashion with the rest of the dough. If you want to dry out the pasta, simply leave it out overnight covered with a dish towel.
- The fresh pasta should cook up in about 2 to 3 minutes. The dried pasta will take about the

same amount of time as the stuff you get at the grocery store.

46. Homemade Pasta With A Lemony Cream, Spinach, And Pea Sauce

Serving: Serves 4 | Prep: | Cook: | Ready in:

Ingredients

- For the pasta
- 3 1/2 cups all-purpose flour
- 1 cup semolina flour
- 5 large eggs
- For the cream sauce
- 1 pint heavy cream
- 2 teaspoons cornstarch
- 1/2 cup grated parmesan
- 1 lemon, juiced
- 2 cups spinach
- 1 cup frozen peas
- 1 pinch salt
- 1 pinch fresh ground black pepper
- 1 tablespoon unsalted butter

Direction

- For the pasta
- Mix the all-purpose flour and the semolina flour in a bowl and until well combined.
- Pour onto a clean surface (or keep in the bowl if you want to keep the pasta dough contained) and create a well in the center of the flour, so that it looks like a volcano.
- Gently whisk your eggs together in a separate bowl, and then pour into the center of the well.
- Slowly pull the flour in from the sides of the well, mixing it with the fork you used to whisk the eggs, or make a swirling motion with your fingers so that the flour is mixed into the egg bit by bit. If some of the egg makes a mad dash for it out of the side of the flour volcano, stop its passage with some flour and guide it back to the middle of the pile.
- When there is enough flour mixed with the eggs so it is not a complete runny mess, knead in the rest of the flour. Knead it for about 5 minutes, or until the dough is silky and elastic.
- Wrap the dough in cling-film and leave it to rest in the fridge for 45 minutes.
- Take it out of the fridge, cut it up into 3-4 portions so it is more manageable, and flatten with your hands.
- Put it through the thickest setting on your pasta maker. Fold it into thirds and repeat. Do this a couple of times -- this is a continuation of the kneading process, making sure that all of the flour and egg is evenly and smoothly combined. Then continue to put it through thinner and thinner settings until your pasta is about 1/16 of an inch thick -- it should be slightly translucent. Then put it through whatever shape cutter you desire -- fettuccini works really nicely with this sauce -- and hang it up to dry for 30 minutes, or, like me, let it dry on the counter, but without all of the strands of pasta touching so that they cling together in a ball. (If you don't have a pasta maker, follow all of these steps but use a rolling pin instead of the pasta maker. When you've reached the desired thickness, lightly flower the surface of the pasta sheet, roll it up, and cut it by hand however you like it.)
- For the cream sauce
- Steam the peas, just enough to defrost them, and set them aside.
- Pour the cream into a pot over a medium heat. Add the cornstarch, whisk, and then the parmesan, and continue whisking together. Heat for five minutes.
- Squeeze in the lemon juice and turn the heat down a bit. Add the salt and pepper, to taste.
- Cook the pasta (if freshly homemade, it will cook in about 3 minutes, if packaged, cook al dente according to package's instructions) and reserve 1/4 cup of the cooking water.
- Return the pasta to the pot and gently toss with the tablespoon of butter until evenly coated. Then coat with the cream sauce and

the reserved cooking water and add in the spinach a handful at a time.
- Serve with the peas on top, along with extra parmesan.

47. Honeyed Greek Filo Custard

Serving: Serves 12 | Prep: | Cook: | Ready in:

Ingredients

- Filo Custard
- 2 cups milk
- 1/2 cup granulated sugar
- 1/4 cup semolina flour
- 1/2 cup unsalted butter
- 1 tablespoon unsalted butter
- 3 eggs, well beaten
- 1 teaspoon finely grated lemon zest
- 1 tablespoon fresh-squeezed lemon juice
- 1/4 teaspoon vanilla extract
- 30 (9 x 14-inch) sheets of filo dough, thawed if frozen
- Honey Syrup
- 1 cup granulated sugar
- 1/4 cup honey
- 3/4 cup water
- 2 tablespoons fresh-squeezed lemon juice

Direction

- Begin by preparing the custard. In a medium saucepot, heat the milk over low heat for 3 minutes, stirring every minute. Add the sugar, semolina flour, and 1 tablespoon of the butter. Continue to cook over low heat, stirring constantly, until the mixture thickens slightly, about 5 minutes.
- In a separate bowl, whisk 1 cup of the milk mixture with the beaten eggs. Pour the egg mixture into the saucepan and whisk constantly for another 3-5 minutes. Remove from heat and whisk in the lemon zest, lemon juice, and vanilla extract until combined. Set aside.
- Preheat the oven to 350 degrees Fahrenheit. Using a small sharp knife, cut an 8-inch diameter circle out of a stack of 10 stack filo dough sheets set them underneath the pile of normal rectangular filo to keep them from drying out. On a flat and clean working surface, lay down one sheet of the rectangular filo dough and lightly brush it with the melted butter. Place the slightly damp towel on the stack of filo dough waiting to be brushed to keep them from becoming dry and brittle. Lay the filo in the cake pan so that the ends hang over the edge of the pan on both sides.
- Use the pastry brush to gently brush the filo against the sides of the cake pan so that it is snug with the corners. Repeat with another layer of rectangular filo, but place it so that it's edges hang off the bare side of the pan, creating a crisscross. Repeat this with 20 sheets of rectangular filo so that the edge of the pan is covered with filo hanging off of it and you cannot see any bare edge.
- Whisk the custard to mix it back up a bit, then pour it into the cake pan. Fold the filo that's been hanging over the edges back over the custard mixture, being careful not to submerge it in the custard. You want it to lay relatively flat over the custard mixture, encasing it. Lightly brush the top with butter.
- Lightly brush a circular filo sheet with butter and place it on top of the folded filo. Repeat until all 10 sheets of the circular filo are on the galaktoboureko. Use the end of a blunt butter knife to tuck the edges of the circular filo down into the pan so the cover is nice and snug. Use a sharp knife to cut 4 small vent holes in the center of the filo, making sure it pierces down into the custard layer, otherwise the air will make the filo rise up into a dome and eventually cause a tear somewhere in the dough.
- Place the pan in the oven and bake for 55 minutes to 1 hour 10 minutes, or until the filo is golden brown and the custard is set
- While the custard is baking, prepare the syrup. Bring the sugar, honey, water, and lemon juice to a boil over medium high heat. Lower the

heat and allot to simmer for 5 minutes, then remove from heat and allow to cool to room temperature, then place in the refrigerator.
- Once the custard is finished baking, remove it from the oven and immediately pour the syrup into the pan over the top of the galaktoboureko. Allow it to soak in the syrup for 1 hour, then slice and serve.

48. Hungarian Stuffed Reds With Red Quinoa

Serving: Serves 4-6 | Prep: | Cook: |Ready in:

Ingredients

- 1/2 cup whole red quinoa, uncooked, soaked in water
- 1/2 pound farm quality ground beef
- 1/2 pound farm fresh quality ground pork
- 1/4 cup finely chopped red cabbage
- 1/4 cup finely chopped red onion
- 1/4 cup grated carrot
- 1/2 teaspoon fresh chopped thyme leaves
- 1/2 teaspoon fresh chopped marjoram leaves
- 1/2 tablespoon premium quality Hungarian smoked (or sweet) paprika
- dash of kosher salt
- pinch of pepper
- 4-6 plump red sweet bell peppers
- 2-4 cups fresh vegetable broth, made from fire roasted as well as uncooked red pepper, tomatoes, carrots, onions and herbs (see photo) with canned stewed tomatoes as alternative
- 1/2 tablespoon sweet red Hungarian paprika
- 1 bay leaf
- 1 bouquet garni of fresh herbs (thyme, marjoram, parsley, even some basil)
- sweet paprika for garnish
- dollop of sour cream, creme fraiche, or fage for serving
- fresh chopped parsley for serving
- 4 cups red pepper semolina soup as a richer alternative to the vegetable broth

Direction

- Soak the quinoa in water for an hour and then drain off the water. Mix gently the next ten ingredients on the recipe list together with the quinoa for the filling.
- Cut a border of triangles out of the top edge of the peppers, about an inch in height. Clean out their seeds and interior membranes. Take the cut out triangles and dice smaller. Add these into the filling mixture.
- Stuff the peppers up to the beginning of the triangular border. The quinoa will expand when cooking.
- Arrange these in a large Dutch oven and add the broth. Make sure to add sweet paprika to the broth. Bring to a boil, then simmer for 40 minutes. While cooking ladle some broth over the peppers. Make sure the quinoa is fully cooked. Remove the peppers carefully to a bowl and peel off their skins, if desired. Replace back into the broth to keep warm until serving. If you do not mind the skins, you can simply skip this step.
- Serve with a generous ladle-ful of broth in a bowl, or alternatively for a richer meal with my red pepper semolina soup. Fold the triangles inwards. Garnish with sour cream, crème fraiche or fage, chopped flat leaf parsley and sweet paprika.

49. Kale Pizza With Blue Cheese And Walnuts

Serving: Serves 4 | Prep: | Cook: |Ready in:

Ingredients

- 2 balls pizza dough (~10 ounces each, preferably whole wheat)
- 2 tablespoons olive oil, plus more for drizzling

- 2 cloves garlic, minced
- 1 bunch kale, if it's really large, or two smaller bunches (I like Red Russian), washed and dried and roughly chopped
- 1 wedge lemon
- Handful flour or semolina, for dusting
- 1/3 cup roughly chopped walnut halves (do not toast, as they'll brown in the oven)
- 1/4-1/3 cups crumbled blue cheese, depending upon your taste
- 1/2 red or yellow onion, sliced into thin half-moons
- salt

Direction

- Preheat your oven, with a pizza stone if you have, to 500 degrees for an hour. If your pizza dough has been refrigerated, let it sit, covered, at room temperature for about the same amount of time.
- While the oven is preheating and the dough is warming, prepare the kale. Heat the olive oil in a large pot over a medium heat. Add the garlic and sauté until starting to brown. Add the kale along with a pinch of salt, and sauté until softened, covering the pot between stirring to help the kale wilt. When it's almost done, squeeze the wedge of lemon over the top and stir to combine. Turn off the heat and set aside.
- Place one ball of the pizza dough on a lightly-floured counter top, and press outward into a thick disk (leaving a 1" unpressed area along the edge as the crust). Pick up the disk and let it drape over the backs of your hands, letting gravity help you stretch it into a 12-14" circle. If the dough resists, let it relax for a few minutes, then try again. Place the stretched dough on a peel (or overturned cookie sheet or cutting board) that's lightly dusted with semolina or other type of flour.
- Take half the sautéed kale, and sprinkle evenly over the dough. Scatter half the walnuts, half the blue cheese, and half the onions on top. Drizzle lightly with olive oil, and sprinkle with a pinch of salt. Slide the pizza onto the preheated stone in your oven, reduce the heat to 450, and bake ~7-10 minutes, until the crust browns. Remove the pizza from the oven, let cool for a moment, and slice into wedges (or, for appetizer servings, cut into squares) and serve.

50. Keeping Cake With Middle Eastern Flavors

Serving: Makes 1 9.5-inch kugelhupf pan | Prep: | Cook: | Ready in:

Ingredients

- 1 cup Pistachios, divided
- 1 cup Butter plus more to grease the pan
- 1/2 pound Cream cheese
- 1 cup Granulated sugar
- 1 teaspoon Vanilla
- 1/2 teaspoon Orange blossom water
- 4 Large eggs
- 1 3/4 cups All purpose flour
- 1/2 cup Semolina
- 1 1/2 teaspoons Baking powder
- 1/2 teaspoon Saffron, crushed
- 1/2 cup Diced dried apricots--pick moist ones!
- 2/3 cup Ground Poppy seeds
- 1/3 cup Granulated Sugar
- 2 teaspoons Orange zest
- 1 teaspoon Orange flower water

Direction

- Grease well the inside of the Kugelhopf pan (I use coconut oil, but butter works as well). Grind half the pistachios and use them to dust the inside of the greased pan, coating all surfaces well. Preheat the oven to 325F.
- In the bowl of a stand mixer, beat together the butter, cream cheese, and sugar until light and fluffy.
- Break the eggs into a bowl, add the saffron to moisten, and add in the vanilla extract and

first amount of orange blossom water. With the mixer at low speed, slip the eggs into the creamed mixture one at a time. Increase speed after each addition until fully incorporated and fluffy.
- Toss the apricots with a Tablespoon of the flour until coated. Sift together the remaining flour, semolina, and baking powder. With the mixer on low speed, add the flour, a quarter at a time. Stop the machine, scrape down the sides, and mix again until the flour us fully incorporated.
- Coarsely chop the remaining pistachios, and fold into the batter along with the apricots.
- In a separate bowl mix the ground poppy seed, sugar, orange zest, and orange flower water, crushing any lumps.
- Spoon a third of the batter into the prepared pan and top with half the poppyseed mixture. Add another third of the batter, and top with the remaining poppyseeds. Spoon on the remaining batter, covering the poppyseeds completely. Rap the pan firmly on the counter two or three times to eliminate any air pockets and smooth the top.
- Bake the cake for 1 1/2-2 hours; start checking for doneness after an hour by sticking a skewer into the deepest part and checking if it comes out clean. If the cake browns too quickly, tent the top with foil.
- Let the cake cool in the pan on a rack for 15 minutes, then carefully unmold and let cool completely on the rack, broad side down.
- Once cooled, wrap tightly in plastic wrap and then in foil. Store in the refrigerator for up to two weeks. Cake also freezes well.

51. Lahm Bi Ajeen

Serving: Serves 8 | Prep: | Cook: |Ready in:

Ingredients

- The Dough
- 1 1/2 teaspoons active dry yeast
- 1/2 teaspoon sugar
- 1 1/2 cups room temperature water, divided into 1 cup and 1/2 cup
- 12 ounces (2 cups) all purpose flour
- 5 ounces (1 cup) 00 flour (or substitute additional all purpose flour)
- 3/4 teaspoon salt
- Topping and Baking
- 21 ounces lean, ground beef
- 2 1/2 tablespoons pomegranate paste/molasses
- 2 tablespoons tomato paste
- 1 banana pepper
- 1/4 cup chopped parsley, loosely packed
- 1/2 small onion, minced
- 3/4 teaspoon salt
- 1/4 teaspoon ground black pepper
- Flour for sprinkling
- Semolina or cornmeal, for sprinkling
- Finishing salt

Direction

- The Dough
- Proof the active dry yeast with the sugar and 1 cup of the water until the water looks a little foamy on top (about 5-10 minutes).
- Add the all-purpose flour, 00 flour, and salt to a bowl (the bowl of a stand mixer, if you plan to knead by machine).
- Add the water/yeast/sugar mixture and stir until the dough starts to come together into a dry, shaggy mess.
- Gradually add a little of the remaining 1/2 cup of water at a time, about 1 tablespoon at a time, until the whole thing comes into a dough ball. Do not use all of the water, unless you need it. If you use too much water, compensate with a little more flour; likewise, if the dough looks too dry, add a little more water and let it sit for a few minutes to absorb. The dough ball should not be too sticky or dry (somewhere in between is best). It should look a tiny bit firmer than store-bought pizza dough.
- Knead until the dough ball passes the window pane test. It should come together into an

elastic ball that has a smooth surface. Kneading should take about 5-15 minutes by machine with a dough hook, or 10-20 minutes by hand. Pay more attention to the dough's consistency than the time you've spent kneading.

- Place the dough in a bowl, cover it, and let it sit at room temperature for 20 minutes, and then in the refrigerator overnight. If you don't have time to wait overnight, you can let it rise at room temperature for 1 1/2 to 2 hours (resting it in the refrigerator will help it develop a better flavor and texture).
- Topping and Baking
- Lightly flour a clean, food-safe work surface, divide the dough into 8 equal pieces, and shape each chunk into a round ball.
- Place a pizza stone (or sheet pan) on the oven floor, move the oven racks up and out of the way, so you can easily access the pizza stone, and pre-heat the oven to 500° F.
- Roll each dough ball into a circle, about 1/8 inch thick. This is very thin, but not paper. Separate the pieces with wax paper and let them rise for about 25 minutes.
- Divide the ground meat mixture into about 8 equal pieces.
- Sprinkle a pizza peel (or rimless sheet pan) with a tablespoon or two of semolina or cornmeal.
- Place a rolled-out disc of dough on the semolina/cornmeal.
- Put one of the pieces of meat on top of the dough disc. Work the meat into a thin, even layer over the dough, so that it doesn't separate from the crust and shrink to the center as it cooks. Sprinkle with a little additional salt, if you'd like.
- Once the oven has preheated, use a quick motion to move the pie from the pizza peel onto the pizza stone. Cook for about 5 minutes, until the meat starts to brown and the bread is cooked through and starting to char.
- Repeat with the remaining 7 pies.

52. Lentils Pancake

Serving: Serves 4 | Prep: | Cook: | Ready in:

Ingredients

- 2 cups Spilt Yellow Lentils
- 2 Dry red chillies
- 1 teaspoon Cumin Seeds
- 2 finely chopped green chillies
- 1/2 cup chopped coriander
- Salt to taste
- 4 tablespoons Semolina
- 4 tablespoons Olive oil
- 5 cups warm water

Direction

- Thoroughly wash the Lentils under running water. Put it into a large bowl and add the dry red chilies, cumin seeds. Mix well and add warm water to cover the Moong fully. Leave overnight to soak.
- Next day, drain the water away; grind the Lentils mixture in a food processor with semolina to get a fine paste. Add water only if required to get the pour-able consistency. Mix in it coriander and salt to taste.
- Heat the pan on medium heat. When hot, add a few drops of oil and mix such that it coats all sides of the pan. Now pour a ladle full of batter onto the pan and spread the batter into a circular shape from the center to outwards. Cook for 1 minute
- Drizzle with a little oil to Pancake to allow oil to go under it. Flip now and cook till the other side is golden too. Remove from pan and serve hot with chutneys of your choice or ketchup

53. MAAMOUL BI FISTOK (PISTACHIO MAAMOUL)

Serving: Makes 40 pieces | Prep: | Cook: | Ready in:

Ingredients

- 2 pounds farina (the very fine semolina)
- 2/3 cup coarse semolina
- 1 1/4 cup all-purpose flour
- 1/2 cup canola oil
- 1 teaspoon active dry yeast
- 1/2 cup orange blossom water
- 1/2 cup rose water
- 1 tablespoon mahleb
- 21 ounces butter, to be clarified
- Filling:
- 1 1/2 cup raw pistachios
- 1/2 cup sugar
- 3 tablespoons orange blossom water

Direction

- Start by clarifying the butter: In a heavy bottomed saucepan, melt the butter over low heat; remove the saucepan from the heat as soon as it has melted. Set aside for 10 minutes. You will notice the milk solids fall to the bottom. Strain it through a wire sieve lined with several layers with cheesecloth. Pour the melted butter over the cheesecloth and get rid of the milk solids. Know you have the clarified butter.
- Mix the farina and coarse semolina in a large bowl. Pour the clarified butter and knead with your hands to infuse all together. Set aside (the semolina mix needs to rest for 6 hours)
- Meanwhile, prepare the filling: place the raw pistachios in a food processor and pulse a few times to considerably grind the pistachios. Transfer to a bowl, add the sugar and orange blossom water, and mix well to fully incorporate. Set aside.
- When 6 hours have passed on soaking the semolina mix, add the all-purpose flour, active dry yeast, mahlab, canola oil, orange blossom water and rose water. Knead the sticky dough for a minute or until the dough is soft and silky. Cover with a kitchen towel and leave it to rest for 1 more hour.
- To put together: Lightly grease a cookie sheet or line it with parchment paper.
- Preheat the oven to 200°C/400°F. Place a rack in the center of the oven
- After 1 hour, knead the dough again and divide it into equal balls, roughly the size of an apricot.
- Make a hole in the center of each ball, with your finger fill the hole with a teaspoon of the pistachio filling. Seal the hole patching the dough together and roll it into a ball.
- Transfer each stuffed ball into the mold, pressing it lightly in to level it up with the mold.
- Gently tap the mold on a counter top, converting it and the maamoul will come out.
- Place it on the cookie sheet, keep the maamoul 2cm/1 inch apart.
- Bake about 15-20 minutes to a golden color. Remove from the oven and set aside to cool down, then dust with powdered sugar. How delicious!!

54. Ma'moul Cookies Cookies Filled With Date Filling

Serving: Makes 2 dozen cookies | Prep: | Cook: | Ready in:

Ingredients

- Shortbread Crust
- 1 cup Butter or vegetable shortening
- 1/4 cup Granulated sugar
- 3 tablespoons Milk
- 1 tablespoon Rose water or you can also use orange blossom water
- 1.5 cups All-purpose flour
- 1/3 cup Semolina
- 1 tablespoon Mahlab ground found at middle eastern stores, they are the small form of almonds found in the seeds of plum. You can use almond instead
- Date Filling
- 1 pound Dates pitted and chopped
- 1/2 cup Sugar, you can definitely decrease a little more sugar as dates are sweet by themselves
- 1/2 cup Water

- 3 tablespoons orange peel or zest of orange
- 1 tablespoon ground almond or mahlab
- Powdered sugar for dusting

Direction

- Shortbread Crust
- Combine 1 cup butter and 1/4 cup granulated sugar in large bowl. Beat at medium speed with electric mixer until well blended.
- Beat in milk and rosewater
- Beat in flour, 1/4 cup at a time until well blended. Add, the semolina and almond meal or mahlab.
- Knead dough in bowl until dough holds together and is easy to shape.
- Date Filling
- Combine dates, water, granulated sugar and almond meal in small saucepan.
- Bring to a boil over medium-high heat. Reduce heat to low; simmer for 4-5 minutes, stirring often, until mixture becomes thick a thick paste.
- Stir in orange peel. Remove from heat, let it cool. (You can also use cinnamon powder, nutmeg or cardamom powder into the filling.)
- To form the cookies - Pinch off walnut sized piece of dough, roll into ball. Pinch sides up to form pot shape.
- Fill center with level tablespoonful of date filling.
- Pinch dough closed, press to seal into a ball. Slightly flatten them and place them on baking sheet with some spacing. Another method is you roll out the pastry dough and cut out cookie shapes with the help of cookie cutter and place them on one cookie and cover it with another cookie and seal it properly and press the edges with fork.
- Place the cookies into a pre-heated oven at 325 F for about 10 to 15 minutes. Do not let them brown. They should light in color but baked well.
- Once done, remove them from oven and place them on a cooling rack for about 2 minutes or so and the sprinkle some powdered sugar if you wish.

55. Mamool

Serving: Makes many! | Prep: | Cook: | Ready in:

Ingredients

- Mamool Dough
- 3 cups fine semolina
- 1/2 cup flour
- 250 to 300 grams butter or soft ghee; exact amount depends on the the how well the semolina absorbs it
- 4 tablespoons milk
- 2 teaspoons mahlab (a spice that can be obtained from any Middle Eastern specialty shop)
- 1/2 teaspoon mastic
- 1/2 teaspoon instant yeast
- 1 cup warm water
- 1/2 cup sugar
- Filling
- Date Filling
- 1/2 cup pitted dates, puréed
- 1 teaspoon mahlab
- 2 teaspoons mamool specialty spices (1 1/2 teaspoons cinnamon, 1 tablespoon ground anise seeds, 1/2 tablespoon mahlab)
- 50 grams butter
- Pistachio or Walnut Filling
- 1/2 cup pistachios or walnuts, well crushed
- 3/4 cup confectioners sugar
- 2 tablespoons orange or rose blossom water

Direction

- Make the filling first: For the date filling, combine all ingredients until a homogenous paste. For the nut filling, mix the nuts with sugar and blossom water until it forms a cohesive dough. Cover and set aside.
- In a bowl, place the semolina and the flour along with a pinch of salt, then add the warm butter or gee, and mix by running fingers through the semolina and making sure the

butter is thoroughly mixed in. Avoid kneading. Cover and set aside for a few hours, allowing the butter to be absorbed by the flour.
- Add the mastic, the mahlab, milk, and sugar to the semolina mixture and mix thoroughly. Adjust sugar to taste.
- Dissolve the yeast in the warm water along with half a teaspoon of sugar and leave for 5 minutes, until bubbling.
- Gradually add the active yeast to the semolina mixture, ensuring gentle mixing with fingers, and not kneading. The dough should be cohesive. The semolina may not need the whole water amount, so add it gradually. Cover the dough and leave aside for 3 hours.
- To form the individual cookies, cut out a portion of the dough that is slightly smaller than the mamool mold. Spread the dough out in a thin layer in the palm of your hand and then place a small portion of the filling into the center of the dough. Wrap the dough around the filling and place in the mamool mold. Press the ball gently into the mold so that the dough fills it completely.
- Turn the mold upside down and gently tap it so that the dough loosens and drops into the palm of your hand. Place the cookie onto a baking sheet that can be covered while the other cookies are being formed to avoid drying. Make sure to leave an inch of space between the cookies to avoid having them stick to each other.
- Bake the cookies at 350° F and keep a close watch. As soon as the dough begins to turn reddish in color, then that's an indication that they cookies are ready.
- Allow for it to cool down completely before removing from the pan to avoid crumbling. Serve by sprinkling powdered sugar on top.

56. Mango Semolina Pudding/ Mango Halwa

Serving: Serves 4 | Prep: | Cook: |Ready in:

Ingredients

- 2 tablespoons Clarified Butter/ Ghee
- 1 cup Semolina/ Rava
- 3/4 cup Sugar
- 1 cup Mango Pulp
- 1/4 teaspoon Cardamon Powder
- 2 1/4 cups Water
- 1/2 cup Ripe Mango chunks (Optional)
- 2 teaspoons Mixed dry nuts (I used cashews, slivered almonds and golden raisins)

Direction

- Heat a pan with clarified butter.
- Fry the mixed nuts until golden brown and reserve for garnish. Care should be taken not to burn it.
- Add the semolina to the pan with clarified butter.
- Roast the semolina until it gives a good aroma.
- Add sugar to the roasted semolina and mix well.
- Now add the water, mango pulp and mix well.
- Make sure there are no lumps by mixing it regularly.
- Cover the pan with lid and cook until the semolina is well done.
- Stir in the ripe mango chunks at this time. This is optional. (I did not add as I did not have some handy)
- Add the fried nuts and serve hot or cold.

57. Marak Kubbeh Adom

Serving: Serves an army. (makes 30 kubbeh) | Prep: | Cook: |Ready in:

Ingredients

- Beet Soup
- Olive oil
- 1 medium onion, roughly chopped
- 6 beets, peeled and roughly chopped
- 4 tablespoons (about 100 grams) tomato puree
- 2 tablespoons sweet paprika
- Salt and freshly ground pepper
- 8 cups chicken stock
- 2 tablespoons sugar
- Juice of 1 lemon
- Marak Kubbeh Adom
- 2 tablespoons olive oil
- 1 tablespoon ras al hanout
- 1 onion, finely chopped
- 3 cloves garlic, minced
- 1 pound lean ground beef
- Freshly ground black pepper
- 3 tablespoons finely chopped cilantro
- 4 cups coarse wheat semolina
- 2 cups water

Direction

- Beet Soup
- Heat olive oil in a large pot over medium heat and sauté the onions until translucent. Add the beets and cook for a few minutes. Stir in the tomato paste. Add the paprika and season with salt and pepper, then add the chicken stock (of course it's best to use homemade here, but just use the best quality you can. I have to admit, I used "chicken soup mix" because that's what we have here, and it turned out great.). Allow to simmer over medium-low heat, uncovered, for at least an hour.
- Just before adding the kubbeh, stir in the sugar and lemon juice. Using an immersion blender, pulse to partially blend the soup (or carefully transfer about 1/3 to a blender). This step is optional and will depend on what texture you like your soup.
- Marak Kubbeh Adom
- Heat the olive oil in a large pan over medium-high heat. Add the ras al hanout and toast, stirring, 1 minute. Add the onions and garlic and sauté until translucent. Add the ground beef and cook, stirring and breaking up with a spoon, until meat is cooked through. Remove from the heat and season with black pepper. If there is a lot of grease and fat in the pan then drain. Allow to cool, stir in cilantro, and set aside.
- Put the semolina and water in a large bowl and allow to sit for a few minutes until the water is fully absorbed. It should be soft, but not liquidy or sticky. Try to avoid adding additional water or semolina as it could become very sticky; if this happens discard and start over. Just trust me.

58. Marillenknödeln With Hazelnut Sauce Apricot Dumplings (Austrian)

Serving: Serves 4 | Prep: | Cook: | Ready in:

Ingredients

- Knödeln
- 3 butter softened
- 1 egg
- 4 tablespoons semolina
- 1 1/3 cups flour
- 250g Quark/very thick Greek yoghurt (1 cup)
- 1 tablespoon vanilla sugar
- 8 apricots
- 8 sugar cubes
- 6 tablespoons breadcrumbs
- 3 ground pistachios or hazelnuts
- 2 1/2 tablespoons powdered sugar
- 1 pinch cinnamon
- 2 tablespoons butter
- Yogurt Hazelnut sauce
- 1/2 cup ground hazelnuts
- 1 teaspoon honey
- 100ml whipping cream
- 1-2 teaspoons vanilla sugar
- 3/4-1 cup plain yoghurt

Direction

- Drain the Quark/Greek yogurt.
- In a bowl, cream the butter, add the egg, semolina and flour. Combine well. Stir in the Quark until you get a thick batter. Set in the fridge for an hour.
- For the sauce, just stir all the ingredients together. Adjust the taste (I like it with a strong hazelnut taste)
- Wash the apricots. With a knife cut the apricots to the middle but NOT in two. Carefully remove the kernels. Replace the kernels with a sugar dice.
- Take the quark mixture out of the fridge. The batter should be quite sticky but if is too sticky, add more flour. Cover your hands with flour and divide the Quark/flour batter into eight pieces/balls. Flatten each ball and wrap the batter around each apricot. Press well to make sure it sticks to the fruit.
- Bring a large bowl of slightly salted water to a boil. Gently plunge each Knödel into the water (use a skimmer) and cook for 12-15 minutes, or until they come to the surface.
- In a skillet on medium heat, melt the butter, then add the breadcrumbs, sugar, pistachios and cinnamon.
- Scoop the Knödel out of the water and immediately roll into the breadcrumb/pistachio mixtures. Put on individual plates and serve with the yogurt sauce.

59. Moroccan Crêpes With Spiced Fruit Compote

Serving: Makes about 10 baghrir | Prep: | Cook: |Ready in:

Ingredients

- For the baghrir:
- 1 1/2 cups semolina flour
- 1/2 cup wheat flour
- 1 1/2 teaspoons dried yeast
- 1 tablespoon baking powder
- 1/2 teaspoon salt
- 1 1/2 teaspoons sugar (I used turbinado, but any sugar is fine)
- 2 cups milk
- 1/4-1/2 cups water
- Unsalted butter, for cooking
- Yogurt, for serving
- Toasted chopped walnuts, for serving
- Honey, for serving
- For the compote:
- 1 cup dates, chopped
- 1 cup dried apricots, chopped
- 2 cups boiling water
- 1/2 teaspoon orange zest, optional
- 2 tablespoons orange juice, optional
- 1/3 cup honey
- 1/4 cup chopped nuts (I used walnuts because that's what I had, but I imagine whole pine nuts would be incredible. Chopped almonds or pistachios would also be delicious!)
- 1/2-3/4 teaspoons ground cinnamon
- 3/4 teaspoon vanilla
- 1/2 teaspoon salt
- 1/4 teaspoon ground cardamom

Direction

- In a large mixing bowl, whisk together semolina, flour, yeast, baking powder, salt, sugar, and milk for the baghrir. Transfer to a blender, and blend for around three minutes; it should be a smooth and relatively thin batter, like that of a French crêpe. Cover and move to the fridge for an overnight rise.
- The next day: pull your batter out of the fridge and make sure it's the desired consistency. It likely will have thickened a bit during fermentation; simply add a tablespoon of water at a time and whisk or blend until it's easily pourable. I ended up adding 5 tablespoons. Allow the batter to rest as you work on the compote.
- In a sauce pan, pour boiling water over the chopped dates and apricots. Cover with a lid, and let soak for 20 minutes.

- Add the rest of the ingredients for the compote to the pot and simmer for 25 to 30 minutes, or until liquid has mostly evaporated and it has become viscous and syrup-y. Remove from heat.
- Heat a non-stick skillet over medium-low heat and melt a dab of butter. Once hot, pour in batter about 1/3 cup at a time, and swirl the pan around to get a thinner coating of batter; these are crêpes, not pancakes! You want a very pale bottom and a just-cooked, sponge-y top. Once the surface is dry, transfer to a plate and cook off the rest.
- Spread a layer of yogurt on top of the crêpe and spoon compote on top. Drizzle with honey or add crushed walnuts if you desire, and serve.

60. Mozzarella, Prosciutto And Olive Salad Stromboli

Serving: Serves 4 | Prep: | Cook: | Ready in:

Ingredients

- The Dough
- 2 ½ teaspoons active dry yeast
- Pinch of sugar, or a few drops of honey
- 2 tablespoons of diced fresh mozzarella
- 2-4 ounces pancetta, cut into small lardons
- 3 tablespoons olive oil, plus more for your hands and the bowl
- 2 tablespoons honey
- ¾ cup diced leftover roasted potatoes (optional, but great if you have them)
- ¾ cup semolina flour
- ¼ cup rye or barley flour (or white, or whole wheat)
- 2 cups white bread flour
- 1 teaspoon salt
- The Fillings, and Assembling and Baking Instructions
- 1 medium yellow onion, or 2 large shallots
- 10 large green olives with pimento
- 8 tablespoons black kalamata olives, pitted
- 2 medium cloves of garlic, peeled
- 4 cornichons
- 1 tablespoon each of fresh marjoram, thyme and basil leaves
- 1 tablespoon finely chopped (not grated) lemon zest (preferably Meyer lemon)   (Or orange zest, but see note below.)
- ¼ cup loosely packed flat leaf parsley
- A splash of red or white wine vinegar
- 1 tablespoon of fruity olive oil
- 8 ounces fresh mozzarella
- 1/4 cup finely grated pecorino romano or parmigiano reggiano
- 4 ounces each of prosciutto and mortadella (or any other Italian deli meats you like)
- Cooked pancetta cubes (left from making the dough)(See note below.)

Direction

- The Dough
- Proof the yeast with a pinch of sugar or a few drops of honey in 3 tablespoons of warm water (no hotter than 110 degrees Fahrenheit).
- In a large skillet, cook the pancetta over medium low heat in 1 tablespoon of olive oil until the pancetta is crispy and has rendered all visible fat. Remove the cooked pancetta and set aside. (You'll use it in the Stromboli filling.)
- Pour off 2 tablespoons of the leftover fat into a measuring cup and add to it one tablespoon of olive oil. Set the skillet aside. (You'll be using it, and whatever fat and oil remains in it, to sauté an onion for the filling.)
- Into a large bowl, put one cup / 236 ml / 236 grams of cold water, the proofed yeast and water mixture, the chopped mozzarella, the olive oil and fat you just measured, and the honey. Stir it well. Add the semolina and rye (or barley, or wheat or white, if you're not using rye) flours, and stir again. Make sure you stir all in the same direction, by the way.
- Add the diced roasted potatoes, if using, the salt and one cup of bread flour. Stir it well to combine.

- Gradually add the remaining flour, mixing it well. At some point, it will become too difficult to stir, so just dump out the contents of the bowl onto your work surface. Scrape whatever is inside the bowl out onto the pile of dough and scraps, and put the bowl in your sink, filled with water, while you knead.
- The dough will seem very sticky, but if you coat your hands with oil, you should be able to handle it without any difficulty.
- Knead until the dough comes together and is fairly smooth. It should take no more than five or six minutes. The potatoes and skins that have come loose will make it a bit lumpy, but don't worry about that.
- Rinse your bowl and dry it well. Drizzle about a teaspoon of olive oil into it and put the dough in. Flip it over to coat it evenly, then top the bowl with a piece of parchment at least twelve inches square. Put a towel over the paper and put the covered bowl in the refrigerator for at least six hours.
- About an hour before using the dough, take it out and let it come to room temperature. It will take less than an hour if you pull the dough apart into smaller pieces. Make sure they are well oiled and covered so they don't dry out.
- N.B. Right after making the dough, you should sauté the onions or shallots, if you want to use the skillet in which you cooked the pancetta. Doing this flavors the onions beautifully, assuming that you like pancetta, of course. See Step 3 below, for more details.
- Also, you can make the dough up to a day ahead of time. Just put it in a plastic bag that you tie off tightly, leaving some room for the dough to rise. Keep it refrigerated until an hour before using.
- The Fillings, and Assembling and Baking Instructions
- Start this process about an hour before you plan to eat. You won't be working on them the whole time, but you need at least a half hour to get your pizza stones or tiles very hot in the oven.
- Preheat the oven, with pizza stones or quarry tiles in the bottom third, to 450 degrees Fahrenheit.
- If you haven't done so already, cook until very light brown the sliced onions or shallots in the skillet in which you cooked the pancetta. Let them sit there until you are ready to use them.
- Chop the olives, the garlic (if using), and the cornichons and combine in a small bowl.
- Without cleaning the surface on which you chopped the olives, finely chop the herbs and citrus zest. Feel free to include a few parsley stems; they're quite flavorful and add a bit of crunch to the mixture.
- Add the herbs to the chopped olive mixture. Add a splash of red or white wine vinegar and the olive oil.
- Cut the fresh mozzarella into 4 inch slices (or 1/2 inch cubes, if using ciliegine).
- Divide the dough into three or four pieces. Shape each into a ball and roll it out into a fairly thin circle that's about 8 to 10 inches in diameter. This dough is full of oil, and it should be nice and stretchy and very easy to handle.
- Put parchment onto a large cookie sheet, preferably one with an open end, off of which you can slide the paper and the uncooked stromboli. You can also work on a pizza peel, of course. If you like using cornmeal or semolina flour instead of the parchment, you can do that, too. I find the parchment on the cookie sheet method to be much easier.
- On one side of each piece of dough, put equal amounts of the olive mixture, then the meat, then the cheese, then a few tablespoons of cooked onion. Sprinkle on a bit of pancetta.
- Fold over and pinch tightly shut.
- About twenty minutes after the oven reaches 450 degrees F, slide parchment paper and the stromboli onto the pizza stones or tiles.
- Cook for about 15 minutes. Let them cool for about five or ten minutes before eating.
- Enjoy!!
- N.B.: If you are not making dough according to the recipe above, i.e., if you haven't already cooked the pancetta by the time you're ready

to assemble stromboli, cook 2-4 ounces of pancetta that has been cut into tiny cubes until it is a bit crispy.
- If using orange zest, substitute finely chopped rosemary leaves for one of the other fresh herbs.

61. ORANGE PATISHAPTA (The Pancake Stuffed With Coconut And Brown Sugar)

Serving: Serves 6 person | Prep: | Cook: |Ready in:

Ingredients

- 200 grams semolina
- 300 grams maida
- 250 grams brown sugar
- 2 cups grated coconut
- 400 liters orange juice
- 5 tablespoons milkmaid
- 3 tablespoons ghee
- 1 piece of eggplant or bottle gourd

Direction

- Condensed milk by constantly billing and stirring, add grated coconut and brown sugar, stir continuously until the mixture attain a thick consistency.
- In a mixing bowl add semolina and maida and pinch of salt and add orange juice gradually to make a thick batter.
- Heat the frying pan and coat the surface of the pan with the little oil. Apply the oil with a piece of eggplant or bottle gourd.
- Pour the batter in big spoon on the hot pan and spread the mix on the pan till it takes a circular shape. Put about the stuffing on the over the spread.
- Roll the spread like bread rolls after 15 -20 second. Keep the roll on the pan and flip sides every 5 - 10 second till the light brown in color.

62. Orange Cake (Portokalopita)

Serving: Serves 12 | Prep: | Cook: |Ready in:

Ingredients

- 3 orange slices
- 2 cups fresh orange juice
- 2 pieces cinnamon sticks
- 1 1/2 cups sugar
- 7-8 cloves
- 1/2 cup extra-virgin olive oil (plus some for greasing)
- some flour for dusting pan
- 4 eggs
- 3/4 greek or strained yogurt
- Orange zest from 1 orange
- 1/2 teaspoon vanilla extract
- 1/2 cup cognac
- 1/4 cup fine semolina
- 1 1/2 teaspoons baking powder
- 1 packet phyllo sheets preferably country-style (thicker)

Direction

- Heat oven to 330°. Put orange slices, 1 cinnamon stick and a few cloves in a baking dish; pour 1 cup orange juice over top. Cover baking dish with foil. Bake until oranges are very soft, 40–45 minutes. Transfer to a rack to cool.
- Meanwhile, bring 3/4 cup sugar, the other cinnamon stick, and 1 1/2 cups water to a boil in a saucepan. Bring to a boil and cook for 4 more minutes; remove from heat. Pour syrup over orange slices. Let cool completely.
- Grease a baking dish and dust with flour. Open the thawed phyllo package. Take each phyllo one-by-one from the short side, crumble it up in your hands and put it in the baking sheet. Use as many phyllo sheets needed to fill up the baking dish. Put them in the oven for 10 – 15 minutes so that they dry up and become slightly crunchy.

- Combine remaining sugar and eggs in a bowl; beat with a hand mixer until pale and thick. Whisk in remaining orange juice, oil, yogurt, zest, cognac and vanilla. In a separate bowl, whisk together semolina and baking powder, whisk into egg mixture. Pour mixture over the slightly pre-baked crunchy phyllo; bake until lightly browned, 35–40 minutes. Pour syrup evenly over cake; let cool. Cut cake into 12 squares and cut orange slices into quarters; top each square with an orange quarter

63. PALLAPPAM (Crisp Laced Rice Pancakes)

Serving: Serves 4 | Prep: | Cook: | Ready in:

Ingredients

- 1 cup Rice Flour
- 1 tablespoon Semolina
- 1/2 cup Water
- 1/2 teaspoon Yeast
- 3 tablespoons Sugar
- 1 1/2 to 2 cups Thick coconut Milk
- 1/4 teaspoon Salt

Direction

- Prepare a thick porridge with the semolina and water. Cool
- Mix together remaining ingredients other than salt; beat in a blender for 2 minutes. (The batter should have a single cream consistency)
- Cover the bowl and prove for 6 to 8 hours
- When double in size, add salt and more coconut milk
- Heat an 'Appam' pan, ladle ¼ cup of the batter into the center of the pan
- Lift the pan and swirl the batter a little bit toward the edge of the pan to get a thin layer of batter around the center
- Cover the pan and cook 4 to 5 minutes till the center is cooked; the edges ought to have a golden brown crust. Usually we have with a spicy curry or a fish molly

64. PINEAPPLE HALWA

Serving: Serves 4 | Prep: | Cook: | Ready in:

Ingredients

- 1 cup Semolina1
- 1 tablespoon Gram Flour
- 1 tablespoon Almond Powder
- 1 cup Ghee or Clarified butter
- 1 cup Sugar
- 5 pieces Tinned Pineapple (2 for Garnishing)
- 12 pieces Raisins
- 12 pieces Almonds, sliced
- 12 pieces Pistachio nuts, sliced
- 3 cups Water
- 1 cup Pineapple syrup
- 1 teaspoon Cardamom Powder
- 1 pinch Saffron

Direction

- 1. Heat ghee or Clarified butter in a pan, add semolina and cook stirring continuously. Add Gram flour & almond powder and stirring till it turns golden brown.
- 2. Boil water, sugar, raisins in a separate pan. Add Pineapple syrup, saffron and cardamom powder and boil. Keep aside.
- 3. Add nuts in the roasted semolina and mix. Add pineapple and further cook for two to three minutes.
- 4. Add boiled water and mix and cover and cook on medium heat for three minutes
- 5. Keep stirring tills all the moisture evaporates and semolina is cooked completely. Garnish with almonds and serve hot on the slice of pineapple.

65. Pasta E Roveja

Serving: Serves 4 | Prep: | Cook: | Ready in:

Ingredients

- For soup
- 1/2 cup roveja - or other dried beans
- 1-2 carrots
- 1/2 onion
- 1-2 celery stalk
- 2-4 garlic cloves
- 1 tablespoon extra virgin olive oil
- hot water
- salt and black pepper
- sage and rosemary, ground
- For pasta
- 2 1/2 cups whole semolina flour
- 1 tablespoon extra virgin olive oil
- 1/2 teaspoon turmeric powder
- 1/4 teaspoon salt
- warm water

Direction

- For soup
- Soak beans as required.
- Mince onion, carrot, celery and garlic. Heat olive oil in a pot and fry veggies for 5-10 minutes, stirring, until translucent.
- Strain and wash very well roveja and add to the pot. Stir and cook for 5 minutes.
- Add some hot water – about 6 cups – and cook until legumes are tender. Add salt, pepper, sage and rosemary.
- For pasta
- In a bowl mix all ingredients and knead until a soft but dry dough is formed. Set aside covered for 30 minutes.
- Roll it on a clean surface – I use a wide wood cutting board – or use a pasta machine. You can use some more semolina flour to dust if the dough is sticky. When the pasta is thin, cut it in irregular shape and let dry a bit.
- When the soup is ready drop maltagliati and let cook for 5-10 minutes. You don't want it to be al dente, but a bit mushy.
- Serve warm and sprinkle with more ground black pepper.

66. Patishapta Indian Crepe With Cardamom Coconut Filling, Drizzled With Date Syrup

Serving: Makes 12 | Prep: | Cook: | Ready in:

Ingredients

- 25 Medjool dates, pitted and roughly chopped
- 4 cups hot water, divided
- 1/8 teaspoon Kosher salt
- 1 cup Dessicated, unsweetened coconut flakes
- 1/4 cup sugar
- 1/4 teaspoon cardamom powder
- 1 pinch Kosher salt
- 1/2 cup Milk (I used 1%)
- 1 cup All purpose flour
- 2 tablespoons rice flour
- 2 tablespoons semolina
- 1/4 cup sugar
- 1 teaspoon Kosher salt
- 2 cups Milk (I used 1%)
- 1/4 teaspoon cardamom powder
- Coconut oil, for cooking

Direction

- Let's make the syrup first! Add the dates and 2 cups of hot water to a glass bowl and microwave on high for 5 minutes. Now pour the mixture in a food processor and add the rest of the 2 cups of hot water. Blend until the mixture is very, very smooth.
- Line a strainer with cheese cloth and strain the date pulp through it. You will have to twist the cheese cloth around the pulp to get most of the liquid out. You should have about 2 cups of liquid after the straining.

- Pour the 2 cups of liquid into a small pot, add 1/8 teaspoon of salt and on medium heat, reduce it until it is about 1/2 cup. Set aside.
- Let's make the filling now! On medium heat, toast the coconut in a small pan until they turn a light golden brown. Add the sugar, cardamom powder, pinch of salt and the milk and cook it until all the liquid is absorbed and the mixture starts getting sticky. Set aside.
- It's time for the crepes! Add the all-purpose flour, rice flour, semolina, sugar, salt and cardamom powder in a bowl and mix well with a whisk. Gradually add in the milk and mix gently to make sure there are no lumps.
- Heat a non-stick sauté pan with a teaspoon of coconut oil on medium heat. Add 1/4 cup of the crepe batter in the middle of the pan (don't swirl it!). It should spread to about 5 inches in diameter by itself. Cook the first side until it gets light golden brown in color (about 2 minutes) and then flip and cook the other side for about a minute or so.
- Once the crepe is done cooking, flip it so that the side that cooked second is facing you. Take a tablespoon of the coconut filling and spread it down the middle. Now fold one side of the crepe and press it down for a second, and then fold the other side and press it down for another second (think of folding a letter).
- Repeat with the rest of the batter. Serve warm, drizzled with the date syrup slightly warmed up.

67. Peach & Tomato Summer Pie

Serving: Serves 4 as appetizer or with sides | Prep: | Cook: | Ready in:

Ingredients

- The crust
- 3/4 cup whole wheat flour
- 1/4 cup semolina flour
- 1/2 teaspoon kosher salt
- 6 tablespoons chilled, unsalted butter cut into small pieces
- 2-4 tablespoons ice water
- The filling
- 2 tablespoons butter
- 1.5 tablespoons sugar
- 1 onion, thinly sliced
- 2 peaches, sliced
- 2 large tomatoes (more if they're smaller), thinly sliced and seeds removed
- 1/2 cup parmesan cheese
- 3/4 cup mozzarella cheese
- 2-5 basil leaves

Direction

- The crust
- Put the flour, semolina, and salt in a bowl (feel free to use a food processor if you have one) and mix.
- Add the butter and mix into the flour until it looks like small peas.
- Add the ice water, 1 tablespoon at a time, until the dough sticks together (when you gather the dough in your fingers and it sticks together without crumbling, it's ready).
- Transfer to a lightly floured board and shape the dough into a disk. Wrap tightly in plastic and refrigerate for at least 30 minutes and up to 24 hours.
- The filling
- Preheat oven to 400 F. Then put a 1/4 inch of water into a pan and heat until boiling. Once boils, add onion and cook for five minutes. Dry onion with a paper towel.
- Add butter and sugar to pan and heat, then add onion. Cook onion for 15-20 minutes to caramelized, watching carefully towards the end so that the onions don't burn.
- Roll out dough on a floured surface so that it is about 1/4 inch thick.
- Arrange alternating slices of peach and tomato (to the best extent possible- definitely won't be as neat as just peach or apple slices, but I promise it will look pretty anyway). Once dough is pretty much covered, fold over the edges. Place in oven for 10 minutes.

- Take pie out of oven, topping with small slices or shredded mozzarella, then adding the caramelized onion. Finally, shred roughly 1/2 cup of parmesan (buy the good stuff- it's worth it) over the top of the pie and place back in the oven for about 15 minutes or until golden brown.
- Place pie on a cooling rack, adding some fresh basil and enjoy.
- If you want, you could definitely add arugula or maybe some balsamic vinegar to this, to really amp up the flavor.

68. Pici Con Le Briciole (Pici With Breadcrumbs)

Serving: Serves 4 | Prep: | Cook: |Ready in:

Ingredients

- For the pici
- 1 1/2 cups (200 grams) plain flour
- 1 1/2 cups (200 grams) semolina flour
- 1 cup (200 milliliters) warm water
- 1 tablespoon extra-virgin olive oil
- For the dressing
- 1/4 cup (60 ml) extra virgin olive oil
- 2 cloves of garlic, chopped
- 4 salted anchovy fillets
- 1/4 cup homemade breadcrumbs
- Salt, pepper and dried chili to taste
- Grated Pecorino cheese, optional
- Fresh parsley, chopped, optional

Direction

- To make the pici, mix the two flours together on a clean surface, forming a pyramid. Create a well in the center of the pyramid and pour in the warm water and oil bit by bit while incorporating the flour by carefully swirling the liquid with your hands. Continue combining the flour and water this way slowly until you get a smooth dough. If you find your dough comes together before you finish incorporating all the flour, stop there; if it is too sticky, dust on some extra flour. You want a ball of dough that springs back when you poke it and no longer sticks to your hands when you roll it. Set the dough aside to rest, covered (in a Tuscan kitchen they simply pop an upturned bowl over it), for at least 30 minutes.
- Separate the dough into two pieces to begin with and on a well-floured surface roll out the first piece until it is about 2 to 3 millimeters (1/10 inch) thick. Cut long strips and then with the palms of your hands or between your thumb and fingers, roll each flat strip from the center outwards, until you have thick noodle, thicker than a spaghetti noodle. Dust with semolina and set aside. Continue until you have finished the dough.
- Heat a pot of water to boil the pasta. If you time all this perfectly, you can prepare the sauce in the very short time that it takes for the pasta to cook. Otherwise, prepare the sauce first -- fresh pasta should never have to wait!
- For the dressing: In a wide skillet, gently sauté the chopped garlic in half of the olive oil until it has softened and is about to turn golden. Add the anchovies and chili and stir until the anchovies melt. Take care not to burn the garlic. Set aside until the pasta has boiled. Prepare your other ingredients.
- Cook the pasta in the boiling, salted water until al dente, about 3 to 4 minutes, depending on the thickness of your pici (taste it: it should be slightly resistant, even chewy, but not taste like flour). Drain, saving some of the cooking water.
- Add the drained pici with a ladleful of the cooking water to the anchovy and garlic mixture in the skillet and over a medium heat toss the pasta for one minute or so, adding the rest of the olive oil and the breadcrumbs, until combined. Serve immediately with some grated pecorino and freshly chopped parsley, if you like.

69. Pizza Rustica

Serving: Serves a lot | Prep: | Cook: | Ready in:

Ingredients

- 2 pounds pizza dough from your favorite recipe
- 1 1/2 pounds sliced cold cuts (ham, salami, turkey, capicola, prosciutto - 3 or 4 types of any you like)
- 1 pound sliced deli cheeses (provolone, cheddar, fontina - 2 or 3 types of your favorite mild cheeses)
- 3 hard boiled eggs, sliced
- 3 beaten eggs, divided
- Semolina or cornmeal for dusting

Direction

- Divide your pizza dough into two pieces, make one slightly larger than the other. The large piece will form your bottom crust and the small, your top crust.
- In a 2-inch deep jelly roll style baking pan (the dimensions should be close to 15X9 for the amount of dough you have), sprinkle the cornmeal or semolina on the bottom. Roll out the larger piece of dough for the bottom crust and lay it in the pan. Let the dough hang over the edges of the pan a bit, similar to when making a pie crust. This will make it easier to seal the top and bottom crust together before baking. Make sure to patch up tears in the dough, if any.
- Begin covering the crust with alternating layers of meats and cheeses. You should have about 3-4 meat layers and 2-3 cheese layers. For the middle layer, add the sliced hard-boiled eggs.
- When the "pie" is full, pour in 2 of the beaten eggs (saving the last one for egg wash).
- Roll out the smaller piece of dough and cover the pie with it. Pinch the edges of the top and bottom crust together to seal.
- Brush the top of the pie with the remaining beaten egg.
- Bake at 375 for approximately 30 minutes, until the top is golden brown. Remove from oven and let cool completely. Slide the pie onto a cutting board and cut into squares.

70. Pizza With Butternut Squash Sauce

Serving: Serves 2 medium pizzas | Prep: | Cook: | Ready in:

Ingredients

- Pizza dough
- 1 cup lukewarm water
- 1/2 teaspoon Dry active yeast
- 1 1/2 teaspoons Kosher salt
- 1 1/2 teaspoons Granulated sugar
- 1 tablespoon Olive oil
- 2 1/2 - 3 1/2 cups Bread flour
- 1/4 cup Semolina or rough cut corn meal
- Butternut squash sauce
- 1 Large butternut squash (frozen works just as well)
- 4 Roma tomatoes or 1 15 oz can of whole or crushed tomatoes
- 2 Large cloves of garlic (or to taste)
- 1 Medium shallot
- 1 teaspoon Kosher salt
- 1/4 - 1/2 teaspoons Cayenne (optional, to taste)
- 1 teaspoon Dried basil (optional)

Direction

- Pizza dough
- Dissolve the yeast, salt, and sugar into the water. Mix in the olive oil.
- Mix in flour with a spoon until you have a soft dough, but not so sticky that it's unmanageable.
- Place the dough in a clean, well-oiled bowl (cooking spray can work well for this) and let sit at room temperature for an hour. Then refrigerate for another hour or as long as

overnight. While the dough is in the fridge, make the sauce and get the toppings ready.
- When ready to make the pizzas, punch down the dough and divide in two. Spread the pizza to the desired size and let rest on a surface dusted with coarse semolina or cornmeal. If you don't have either of these, then flour works fine as well, though I like the rough texture that the semolina provides.
- Butternut squash sauce
- If using a fresh squash, cut it in half, lightly rub with olive oil, and roast at 350 degrees F until easily pierced with a fork at the thick ends (~30 - 45 minutes). Also roast the roma tomatoes if using fresh ones (so that the skin is easy to remove).
- When soft, scoop the squash from the skin with a spoon. Place in a bowl.
- Skin the roast tomatoes or open the can of tomatoes.
- Dice the garlic and shallot and fry in a little bit of oil (2 - 3 tsp) until translucent or very lightly browned. If you don't have a food processor, do this step in a medium sauce pan.
- The next step can be done one of two ways: If you have a food processor, add all the ingredients to the food processor and make a puree. If you don't have a food processor, add all remaining ingredients to the pan with the garlic and shallots and squish the squash and tomatoes into a sauce with the back of a wooden spoon. Let simmer until it looks well combined. I've never been a fan of oregano or thyme, but if you like those, you could add those here. If I didn't have fresh basil to put on top of the pizza, I might be inclined to mix some into the sauce at this point.
- Now the sauce is ready to use! Simple toppings will allow you to taste the sauce more, but it works equally well with flavorful toppings. It is topped with 3/4 units shredded mozzarella, 1/4 unit shredded parmesan, blobs of herb-encrusted goat cheese, anchovies, and spinach leaves (which I put under the cheese so it doesn't get dried out when I bake it)

- Bake the pizza at 400 - 450 F on a pizza stone for about 15 - 25 minutes, or until the cheese is nicely browned. Cooking time will depend partly on how much topping you put on the pizza (less is often more).

71. Revani, Syrup Soaked Semolina Cake

Serving: Makes 9 squares | Prep: 1hours0mins | Cook: 0hours45mins | Ready in:

Ingredients

- Syrup
- 2 cups water
- 1 cup and 2 tbsp sugar
- Juice of a lemon, lime or 1/2 an orange
- Optional - a few strips of lemon, lime or orange peel
- Cake
- 1/2 cup all purpose flour plus 1 tbsp cornstarch
- 1/2 cup semolina
- 1 tablespoon baking powder (yes all that, equivalent to 3 tsp)
- 1/2 cup sugar
- 4 large eggs, room temperature
- 1 tablespoon extra virgin olive oil
- 1 teaspoon pure vanilla extract
- 1/4 teaspoon grated zest of a lemon, lime, or orange

Direction

- Syrup
- Grease an 8" x 8" square cake pan. Preheat oven to 375 deg. F. Combine all syrup ingredients, bring to a boil and let it simmer for 10 minutes and take off heat and set aside. Note that this syrup is more on the thin side due to the water/sugar ratio of 2:1 rather than 1:1. I thought to decrease the water from 2 to 1 1/2 cups to make the syrup thicker; but I think

this would make the cake sweeter than what it needs to be.
- Cake
- In a bowl mix together the semolina, flour, cornstarch, and baking powder and set aside. Using a hand or standalone mixer, mix until well combined the sugar, eggs, oil, vanilla, zest and eggs. Add the flour mixture to the wet ingredients and mix until all ingredients are well incorporated. Pour into greased 8x8 square cake pan, and bake for 25 to 30 minutes, or until a toothpick inserted in the middle of the cake comes out clean. It took me 25 minutes. Let cake cool in pan for ½ hour to 1 hour, then cut into 9 squares, and slowly pour the syrup into the cake. You can serve immediately or wait until the following day, as many think it is best the day after. You can serve as is or with a dusting of ground pistachios, and/or grated coconut flakes, and/or whipped/clotted cream.
- NOTE: Semolina is the coarse, purified wheat middling of durum wheat used in making pasta, breakfast cereals, puddings, and couscous. The one I used was given by my mother and found in the Latin American section of a supermarket. But you can also find it (I think) either in the pasta or baking section.

72. Ricotta Gnocchi Served With Blueberry Compote

Serving: Serves 4 | Prep: | Cook: |Ready in:

Ingredients

- For the Gnocchi
- • 1 1/2 cups (12 ounces) whole milk ricotta, homemade or purchased, drained for at list 4 hours or overnight
- • 2 large egg yolks
- • 3/4 cup "00" flour or all-purpose flour
- • 2 tablespoons semolina (which is used for cooking Cream of Wheat, not flour)
- • 2 teaspoons sugar
- • 2 teaspoons grated lemon zest
- • 1/4 teaspoon salt
- • 1/2 teaspoon cinnamon
- • Melted or browned butter for serving
- For the Blueberry Compote
- • 1/2 cup red wine
- • 1/4 cup sugar
- • 1 pound fresh organic blueberries
- • Juice from 1/2 lemon
- • 1 teaspoon vanilla extract
- • 2 teaspoons any berry liqueur you have

Direction

- For the Gnocchi
- To make the Gnocchi: In a large bowl, using a large fork, mix well ricotta until smooth; add egg yolks, lemon zest, sugar, salt and cinnamon; mix until combined.
- Sift flour over the mixture; sprinkle semolina and using a rubber spatula gently fold together.
- Turn mixture out onto a lightly floured work surface. Lightly knead just until dough comes together (do not overwork dough).
- Divide the dough into 4 pieces, and roll into 1/2-inch-thick ropes on a floured surface. Cut each rope into 1/2-inch pieces, deep your finger tip in flour and make an indentation in each gnocchi. Place on a lightly floured baking sheet. Keep in the refrigerator until ready to use.
- For the Blueberry Compote
- In a medium sauce pan bring wine and sugar to boil, add the blueberries, bring back to boil, reduce to simmer and cook on low heat for 5-7 minutes; add lemon juice, vanilla extract and liqueur; cook 1 more minute.
- To serve: Bring a large pot of salted water to a boil, shake off excess flour from gnocchi add to boiling water. Cook until they plump up and float to surface, 2-3 minutes. Drain, shake off excess water and toss in a large bowl with melted butter.

- Divide the gnocchi between serving plates; spoon the blueberry compote on top, add a few fresh blueberries, eat and enjoy!

73. Ricotta Feta Gnocchi Tossed In Maple Brown Butter And Sweet Peas Sauce

Serving: Serves 4 | Prep: | Cook: | Ready in:

Ingredients

- For the Gnocchi
- • 1 cup (8 ounces) whole milk ricotta, homemade or purchased, drained for at list 4 hours or overnight
- • 1/2 cup (4 ounces) best quality French or Greek feta
- • 2 extra- large egg yolks
- • 3/4 cup "00" flour or unbleached all-purpose flour
- • 2 tablespoons semolina (which is used for cooking Cream of Wheat, not flour)
- • 2 teaspoons grated lemon zest
- • Coarse salt and finely ground black or white pepper
- • 1/4 teaspoon freshly grated nutmeg
- For the Maple-Brown-Butter
- • 4 tablespoons (1/2 stick) unsalted butter
- • 1/4 cup pure maple syrup (preferably grade B)
- • 1/2 teaspoon coarse salt
- • 1 sprig of fresh thyme
- • 2 teaspoons lemon juice
- • 1 cup sweet green peas, fresh or frozen and thawed
- • About 2 teaspoons lemon zest, for serving
- • 2 teaspoons fresh thyme leaves, for serving
- • Freshly grated Parmigiano Reggiano

Direction

- For the Gnocchi
- To make the Gnocchi: In a large bowl, using a large fork, mix well ricotta and feta until smooth; add egg yolks, lemon zest, salt and pepper, mix until combined. Sift flour over the mixture; sprinkle semolina and using a rubber spatula gently fold together.
- Turn mixture out onto a lightly floured work surface. Lightly knead just until dough comes together (do not overwork dough).
- Divide the dough into 4 pieces, and roll into 1/2-inch-thick ropes on a floured surface. Cut each rope into 1/2-inch pieces, deep your finger tip in flour and make an indentation in each gnocchi. Place on a lightly floured baking sheet; cover with a kitchen towel. Transfer to the refrigerator until ready to use.
- For the Maple-Brown-Butter
- To make the Maple-Brown-Butter: In a small saucepan, heat butter over medium heat, swirling pan occasionally, until golden brown and most of the foam has subsided, 8 to 10 minutes. Immediately strain into a small bowl.
- In a clean saucepan, bring maple syrup, salt and the thyme sprig to a boil over medium-high and cook 2 minutes; then discard thyme sprig, add brown butter and mix in lemon juice and peas. Cover and keep warm over a pot of simmering water.
- To serve: Bring a large pot of salted water to a boil, shake off excess flour from the gnocchi and add to boiling water. When they plump up and float to surface, lower the heat and cook for about 3-4 minutes. Drain, shake off excess water and toss with the Maple-Brown-Butter and Peas Sauce in a large bowl.
- Transfer to a warmed platter or individual bowls, sprinkle with thyme leaves, lemon zest and grate Parmigiano Reggiano over the top. Serve immediately.

74. Roasted Carrot Soup With Meyer Lemon And Rosemary

Serving: Serves 2-4 | Prep: | Cook: | Ready in:

Ingredients

- 1/2 tablespoon unsalted butter or ghee
- 2 tablespoons olive oil
- zest from 1 Meyer lemon
- 2 teaspoons minced fresh rosemary leaves
- 1/2 tablespoon sweet Hungarian paprika
- 1 teaspoon Maldon salt flakes, to taste
- 1/4 teaspoon fresh milled pepper
- 1/4 cup semolina
- 2 cups fresh carrot juice, divided
- 3/4-1 cups roasted carrot, pureed
- 2 roasted garlic cloves, pureed
- 1/4 cup roasted parsnip, pureed, optional
- 1/4 cup roasted onions, pureed, optional
- 1 egg
- 1/2 cup buttermilk, plus more for thinning soup, if desired
- 1/2 cup dry white wine, optional
- juice from 1 Meyer lemon (or 2)
- rosemary sprigs for garnish, optional
- chiffonade of basil or mint for garnish, optional
- slices of warmed roast carrot for garnish

Direction

- In a heavy pan melt the butter or ghee. Add the spices, herbs, zest, salt, and pepper. Pour in the olive oil and continue to heat. Stir in the semolina and take off the heat.
- Puree the vegetables with one half of the carrot juice. Then pour in the puree mixture into the pan. Return to the pan to heat. Keep stirring until everything comes together. Stir in the remaining carrot juice. Test for seasoning and adjust.
- Whisk the egg with the buttermilk. Slowly add that to the pan, whisking it in. (If you prefer, you can temper the egg mix first before adding to the warm mix.) Keep stirring and bring to a slow simmer. After 5-10 minutes, add the optional wine; stir in the Meyer lemon juice. Add a little more buttermilk, wine and/or lemon juice if you want to thin the soup. Cook for just a few minutes more.
- Ladle into bowls. Garnish with warm roasted carrots, rosemary leaves, basil or mint leaves.

75. Rye Orecchiette With Stinging Nettles, Sheep's Milk Feta, And Chive Blossoms

Serving: Serves 6 | Prep: | Cook: | Ready in:

Ingredients

- 1 1/2 cups plus 1 to 3 tablespoons (about 165 grams) rye flour
- 1 1/2 cups (about 280 grams) semolina flour, plus more for shaping
- 3 teaspoons kosher salt
- 1 cup warm water, plus 1 to 3 tablespoons if needed
- 1/4 cup olive oil, plus more as needed
- 1 shallot, chopped roughly
- 5 cloves garlic, chopped roughly
- 1/2 pound nettles, stems removed (about 7 to 8 cups, or 4 ounces, loosely packed leaves)
- Salt and freshly ground pepper, to taste
- 1/2 to 3/4 cup chicken or vegetable stock
- 1/4 cup reserved pasta liquid, plus more as needed
- 8 ounces sheep's milk feta cheese
- Zest from 1/4 lemon
- Chive blossoms or fresh snipped chives, for garnish

Direction

- In a large mixing bowl, combine the rye flour, semolina flour, and salt. (If mixing in the bowl of a stand mixer, use the dough hook attachment.) Add 1 cup of warm water and combine on medium speed (or using a spatula), until a ball of dough forms and pulls away from the sides of the bowl. If you notice the dough crumbling, add 1 to 3 more tablespoons of warm water. If you notice that it's too sticky, add 1 to 3 more tablespoons of rye flour until it loses its stickiness.

- Knead the dough until it becomes smooth and supple. If you're using a stand mixer, this will take about 5 to 6 minutes on medium speed; if you're using your hands, it will take a bit longer, about 8 to 10 minutes. The dough should be cohesive and smooth after kneading. Wrap the dough in plastic wrap and allow to rest in a dry place at room temperature for 45 minutes.
- Once the dough has rested, lightly dust your workspace with about 1 tablespoon of semolina flour. Wooden work surfaces, such as butcher block countertops or large wooden boards, are ideal for shaping the orecchiette. Use the dusting flour sparingly; 1 to 2 tablespoons should be enough for the entire mass of dough. Dust 2 large rimmed baking trays with semolina flour sparingly, about 1 tablespoon per tray.
- Cut off approximately one-sixth of the dough (about 100 grams) and roll into a long rope that's about 1/2-inch in diameter. Cut the log into several small pieces, about 1/2-inch wide, and one by one roll each piece into a circle. To give you a sense of how large these should be, 5 orecchiette pieces (uncooked) should weigh about 12 to 15 grams. On the dusted work surface, press down with your finger into the center of each dough circle (I use my middle finger, but you could also use your thumb) and rotate in small circles to spread the dough into a bowl shape, making it thin at the bottom. Next, pinch each dough piece on your finger to smooth out the shape. To get the classic orecchiette shape, pull back on the edges to create a small ear-like saucer. Place the finished orecchiette on the dusted baking tray and continue the process until all of the dough is formed into orecchiette. Make sure not to allow them to touch on the tray or they will stick together.
- The formed orecchiette can be frozen directly on the trays and then transferred and stored in sealed storage containers in the freezer for up to 2 to 3 weeks. Cook the frozen orecchiette just as you would the fresh; do not thaw before cooking.

- In a large pot, heat 1/4 cup of olive oil over medium heat. Add shallots and cook until translucent, about 4 to 5 minutes. Add garlic and cook until fragrant, about 2 minutes. Add nettles, salt, and pepper, and cook, stirring frequently, until nettles have wilted, about 5 to 6 minutes. Add the stock and continue to cook, 1 to 2 minutes.
- Transfer to a bowl and blend with an immersion blender, or purée in a food processor until smooth. Set aside.
- Bring a large pot of salted water to a gentle simmer. Add all the orecchiette at once and cook until you notice them floating to the top, about 3 to 4 minutes. Once they've floated to the top, continue to cook approximately 2 to 3 minutes longer or until al dente. Reserve 1 cup of pasta liquid for later use and drain cooked orecchiette in a colander.
- Toss cooked orecchiette with the nettle purée and 1/4 cup of the reserved pasta liquid, adding a little bit at a time until you've reached your desired ratio. If you have leftover purée, you can freeze it in ice cubes for several weeks for later use.
- Toss the finished pasta with the feta and lemon zest, then garnish with fresh herbs. I used chive blossoms here for their delicate flavor, but fresh-snipped chives or basil would also work well.

76. SCALLION PANCAKE WITH PEANUT COCONUT TAMARIND CHUTNEY

Serving: Makes 6 - 8 pieces | Prep: | Cook: | Ready in:

Ingredients

- Pancakes
- 2 Stalks of Scallion
- 1/2 teaspoon Maple Syrup
- 1 cup Semolina (Fine)
- 1/2 cup Yogurt

- 1 teaspoon Salt
- 1/2 teaspoon Baking Powder
- 1/2 teaspoon Oil (any kind)
- Peanut Coconut Chutney
- 1/2 cup Roasted Peanuts
- 1/2 cup Shredded Coconut
- 1 teaspoon Tamarind paste
- 1 piece Green Chilli or red chilli
- 2 tablespoons Coconut Cream
- 1/2 teaspoon Sugar
- 1/2 teaspoon Salt (start with little and then add acc to taste)

Direction

- In a bowl, mix semolina, yogurt, baking powder and salt. Add some water to make a paste consistency. Keep the bowl in a warm place to ferment for 20-25 minutes. In a blender mix all the ingredients of chutney and blend until smooth. Keep it on the side.
- Thinly sliced the scallions both white and the green part. In a small pan, warm oil scallion and maple syrup and a little salt; cook for 5 minutes on a medium flame.
- Warm the pancake mold and coat it with oil. Put 1 tablespoon of semolina mix, add 1/2 teaspoon scallions and then another tablespoon on the top. Repeat it for the rest of the mixture.
- Cook for 3 - 5 minutes and then use a toothpick to turn the cakes after 5 minutes or once it gets brown from the bottom. Apply some oil if needed. Let it brown from both the sides before taking them off.

77. SEMOLINA WITH TOASTED SEEDS AND VEGETABLES

Serving: Serves 4 | Prep: | Cook: |Ready in:

Ingredients

- 150 grams pre-cooked green soybeans
- 50 milliliters olive oil
- 3 tablespoons sunflower seeds
- 3 tablespoons pumpkin seeds
- 3 tablespoons poppy seeds
- 2 garlic cloves
- 300 grams semolina
- 3 carrots
- 1 tablespoon honey
- 1 zest of a lime
- 1 juice from 1/2 a lime
- feta
- parsley
- salt and pepper

Direction

- In a hot pan, heat the olive oil with the garlic cloves (previously cut them into the small pieces) and add the seeds.
- Warm for 5 minutes or until the garlic turns brown. Do not hesitate to mix it time to time.
- Meanwhile, peel and cut the carrots into the slices.
- Put them into the pan, add the honey, the juice, and zest of a lime. Stir and heat for 8-10 more minutes.
- In a baking dish, put the semolina and pour little by little some hot water. Previously at home, we already cooked the green soybeans so we pour the same water to the semolina but you can also boil the new water in a saucepan and add a cube of vegetable broth as well. The water amount depends on the semolina, it needs to absorb it all. Do not hesitate to taste it. :p
- Stir with a fork.
- Add some feta which you sprinkle with your hands.
- The finishing touch is to put also some chopped parsley, salt, and pepper. Et voila!

78. SEMOLINA YOGURT ROSE PETAL CAKE/ROSE FLAVOURED BASBOUSA

Serving: Serves 20 | Prep: | Cook: | Ready in:

Ingredients

- For the cake :
- 1 cup Semolina/farina (the roasted variety is preferable or roast the semolina on low heat till golden brown)
- 3 tablespoons All purpose flour
- 4 Eggs
- 1 teaspoon Rose Essence
- 1/4 teaspoon Salt
- 1/2 cup Chopped,salted Pistachios
- For the syrup :
- 1 cup Sugar
- 1 cup Water
- 1/2 tablespoon Lemon Juice

Direction

- For the cake:
- Preheat oven to 180°C. Prepare the baking tray – Brush the insides with oil and line it with butter/parchment paper.
- Mix eggs and sugar in a bowl and beat with a hand blender till soft and creamy. Add the yogurt, salt and oil and blend well to combine all the ingredients. Add both vanilla and rose essence and mix well.
- Now mix in the semolina, all-purpose flour, baking powder and soda. Keeping 2 tbsp. of each for sprinkling on top add the Pistachio and crushed Rose petals and fold with a spatula till all the ingredients are amalgamated.
- Pour into the prepared pan and thump the tray on the kitchen countertop to remove any air bubbles. Sprinkle the leftover nuts and petals on top.
- Bake in the preheated oven for 25 – 30 minutes till golden brown on top.
- Remove the cake from the oven and immediately pour on the prepared and cooled syrup evenly over the cake. The semolina will soak up the syrup quickly and you will be left with a delicious soaked cake. However do not remove the cake now as it will be very delicate with the soaking it got.
- Cover the cake with foil or Clingfilm. I put the whole tray in a slider bag and put it in the refrigerator for 24 hours. You can also put it in a food grade plastic storage bag. By this time it would firm up and it would be easy to cut and store.
- Cut the cake into neat slices. Let it come to room temperature and serve as liked.
- For the syrup:
- Heat the water and sugar together till sugar dissolves and the liquid starts boiling. Take off heat and add the lemon juice. Cool to room temperature.

79. SUJI HALWA

Serving: Serves 4 | Prep: | Cook: | Ready in:

Ingredients

- 1 cup suji (semolina flour)
- 1 cup sugar
- 5 tablespoons butter*
- 6 green cardamom pods
- 2 tablespoons almond slivers
- 1 tablespoon golden raisins
- 1 teaspoon pistachios, for garnish

Direction

- *Note that the recipe generally calls for 8 tablespoons of ghee (clarified butter), so if you keep ghee on hand, go for it. I don't, so we used regular butter instead. And since I figured I'd end up eating a lot of the batch myself (as per usual), I opted for 5 tablespoons instead of 8, which makes for the yummy, more crumbly texture shown here.
- Crush cardamom pods with mortar and pestle to separate the pods from the seeds. Set aside.

- Add 2 cups water, plus sugar and cardamom pods (not seeds) to saucepan on medium-high heat. Let water come to a full boil, stirring occasionally to ensure sugar melts into the water. Then reduce heat to medium-low and let it continue to boil gently.
- In a large frying pan, dry roast suji on medium heat until light brown and fragrant, stirring constantly. This will take 2 to 4 minutes.
- Add butter, cardamom seeds and 1 tablespoon almonds to frying pan and cook for another 2 to 4 minutes until the butter is fully incorporated into the semolina, stirring constantly.
- Reduce saucepan heat to low and remove cardamom pods. Slowly add water-sugar mixture to frying pan little by little (since it will sizzle), stirring often. Continue to cook and stir for 2 to 4 minutes. It's done when the water is absorbed and the halwa mixture separates in a mass and leaves some butter visible at the sides of the pan.
- Let cool just a tad and scoop into dishes. Then crush pistachio with mortar and pestle and use it to garnish, along with remaining almond slivers.

80. Sardinian Clam Stew With Fregola

Serving: Serves 3 | Prep: | Cook: | Ready in:

Ingredients

- Fregola
- 1 1/4 cups (200 grams) semolina or durum wheat flour
- 1 egg yolk
- 1/3 cup water, or as needed
- 1 pinch salt
- 1-2 tablespoons all-purpose flour
- Clam Stew
- 2 pounds (1 kg) clams
- 1 garlic clove, finely chopped
- 1 small onion, finely chopped
- 1 handful parsley, finely chopped
- 3 tablespoons extra virgin olive oil
- 1/2 cup dry white wine
- 1 cup (250 ml) tomato passata (you can also substitute with a whole fresh tomato, chopped)
- 1 cup water or as needed

Direction

- Fregola
- Pour the semolina flour into a wide shallow ceramic bowl or onto a wooden surface (wood is an ideal material for this as it tends to add some traction as you rub the liquid into the egg).
- Combine the yolk, water, and salt in a small bowl. Dribble a teaspoon of the egg mixture onto the semolina, and with the fingertips of one hand, drag the liquid through the semolina to create little, irregular-shaped balls. Dribble and drag, rubbing the egg mixture into the flour in a circular motion, until all the flour or all the egg is used up. If you find the mixture feels too moist, a spoonful or two of regular flour can be added to avoid clumping.
- Heat oven to 150° C/300° F. Place the fregola in a single layer on a baking tray and bake for about 10-15 minutes, or until they feel dry to the touch. You can also leave them out, uncovered, for several days to dry naturally. Let cool.
- Clam Stew
- Rinse the clams and remove any with broken shells. If you need to purge the clams (if they haven't already been purged and de-sanded where you bought them), at about 1 hour before you plan on cooking them, place the clams in a large, wide shallow dish such as a lasagne tray, cover with an inch of salt water (for 4 cups of fresh water, 2 tablespoons of salt, which is similar to the salinity of seawater). Let the clams purge 1 hour at most. Discard the water, being careful not to pour the filtered grit back over the shells. In a wide skillet, open the clams over high heat. A tight-fitting lid

helps this along, it should take a few minutes of shaking the pan to move them around and let the ones on the bottom come to the top to open. When they've opened, turn off heat and strain the liquid produced from the clams — set this aside. Remove the clams from their shells (save a handful in their shells for garnish, if you like). Set aside.

- In the same pan, sauté the garlic, onion, and parsley with the olive oil over low heat until the onion is translucent and soft. Add the white wine and turn the heat to medium-high. Let the alcohol cook off for a few minutes, then add the tomato, along with the clam water. Bring to the boil then turn down to a low simmer. Let cook for about 10 minutes. Taste and add salt and pepper if needed.
- At this point, you can add the fregola (you can also use store-bought fregola, though you may need to check the cooking times recommended on the packet), along with 1 cup of water or as needed. Bring to a boil, then turn down to a low simmer and cook, uncovered, for 10-12 minutes or until the fregola is cooked through. You are looking for a mixture that is the texture of risotto — soupy but not too stiff/solid. You may need to add a splash of water if the mixture gets too thick and the fregola are still too al dente. Add the clams at the very end to heat through, then serve immediately.

81. Savory Vegetable Cake

Serving: Serves 6 - 8 people | Prep: | Cook: | Ready in:

Ingredients

- Savory Vegetable Cake
- 1 cup coarse semolina flour
- 1/2 cup chickpea flour
- 1 cup yogurt
- 1/4 cup olive oil
- 1 tablespoon baking powder
- Dice following vegetables finely
- 1 carrot
- 1 small potato
- 1 small onion
- 1 red bell pepper
- 2 scallions
- 1/2 cup peas
- 1/2 cup shredded cabbage / shredded zucchini
- 1/2 cup cilantro leaves
- 1 juice of lemon
- 2 tablespoons honey
- 1 tablespoon salt
- Pound following ingredients in a pestle mortar/food processor to paste.
- 2 garlic cloves
- 1 inch ginger piece
- 3 small green chillies
- 1 tablespoon cumin
- For tempering
- 2 tablespoons ghee/coconut oil
- 1 teaspoon cumin seeds
- 1 teaspoon mustard seeds
- pinch asafotida/Hing - Optional

Direction

- Preheat the oven to 375°F.
- Peel the carrot, potato and onion, dice them finely along with red bell pepper and scallions. Add peas and shredded cabbage or zucchini to the mix. Also add chopped cilantro leaves.
- Pound garlic, ginger, green chillies and cumin seeds in a pestle mortar/food processor to paste.
- Mix semolina flour, chickpea flour and baking powder in a large bowl. Add yogurt and olive oil and mix well.
- Add all the vegetables to the batter along with garlic-ginger-chili paste. Add lemon juice, honey and salt. Mix well, batter should be thick at this point.
- Next, heat 2 tbsps. ghee, add the mustard seeds and let them pop (it will make popping sound). Now add the cumin seeds and asafoetida/hing, cook for only few seconds. Add this to the batter.

- Add 1/4 cup of hot water to the batter and mix thoroughly with a wooden spoon. Pour the batter in the oil greased cake pan. Sprinkle generous amount of sesame seeds on top. Place in the centre of the oven for 15 minutes than reduce the temperature to 300°F for another 45-60 minutes until cake has a dark brown color and toothpick comes out clean. Remove from the oven and cool in the pan for 30 minutes. Take the cake out of the pan, cut into slices and serve warm or cold.
- This dish will stay well in the fridge for up to 3 days.

82. Semolina Crackers With Baked On Goat Cheese

Serving: Makes makes about 2 dozen crackers | Prep: | Cook: | Ready in:

Ingredients

- 1 cup (163 g) semolina flour
- 1 cup (120 g) all purpose flour
- 3/4 teaspoon (3 g) fine sea salt
- 2 tablespoons (24 g) extra virgin oil, plus more for finishing
- 1/2 cup plus 1 tablespoon (127 g) cool water
- 4 ounces (113 g) goat cheese
- 2 shallots, peeled and very thinly sliced
- freshly ground black pepper

Direction

- In the bowl of an electric mixer fitted with the dough hook attachment, mix the semolina, all-purpose flour, salt, olive oil, and water for 2 minutes on low speed.
- Raise speed to medium and mix for 1 minute more. Wrap the dough tightly in plastic wrap and let rest at room temperature for 15-20 minutes.
- Preheat the oven to 450°F. Line two baking sheets with parchment paper.
- On a lightly floured surface, roll out the dough to ¼ inch thick. Use a pastry wheel to cut into 2 x 2 inch squares.
- Transfer the squares to the prepared baking sheets (they won't spread so they can be relatively close together). Dock each square 1 or 2 times with the tines of a fork.
- Top each cracker with some goat cheese (about 1 heaping teaspoon per cracker), and a few slices of shallot. Drizzle a little olive oil over the shallots and top with pepper.
- Bake the crackers until they're golden at the edges and very crisp, 10-12 minutes. Let cool at least 5 minutes before serving warm, or cool completely.

83. Semolina Dumplings

Serving: Serves 6-8 | Prep: | Cook: |Ready in:

Ingredients

- • 3 ½ cups of water (for soups) or milk (for serving as a mane dish)
- • 1 cup semolina
- • 2 tablespoons butter, plus 3 tablespoons browned butter for serving
- • 5 large eggs room temperature
- • 1 teaspoon granulated sugar
- • ½ teaspoon salt
- • 1 tablespoon chopped parsley or Basel (for cooked in soups)
- • 1/4 teaspoon freshly grated nutmeg (for the mane dish)

Direction

- In a medium sauce pan bring water or milk, butter, sugar and salt to a simmer. Slowly pour semolina, while whisking, into the pan. When the semolina is incorporated, and there are no lumps, change the whisk to a wooden spoon. Cook constantly stirring for about 8 to 10 minutes. Take the pan of the stove, let it cool slightly, and then stir in the eggs (one at

the time) like for the Pate Choux dough. When the dough is smooth and homogeneous, wet your hands in cold water, and form small canals or balls, lower to a pat with boiling slightly salted water. When the water comes back to a boil; turn down the flame to medium-low. When dumplings come up to the surface, cook them not more than for 5-7 minutes.
- In a small sauce pan slowly brown the 3 tablespoons butter. Cook in portions, don't overcrowd the pat. Take the dumplings carefully out with a strainer, and gently shake of the excess water. Transfer dumplings to a pretty shallow bowl, and pour the browned butter over them. Serve immediately.
- I put on the table grated cheeses, such as good quality Parmesan, Gruyere, or blue cheese; in small nice sauce bowls sour cream or crème fraiche, and also macerated fresh berries, and preserves for my guests, who likes the dumplings more as a dessert.

84. Semolina Pancakes With Spicy Merguez Filling

Serving: Serves 6-8 depending on serving size | Prep: | Cook: |Ready in:

Ingredients

- Pancakes
- 3 cups warm ricotta whey or water or low fat milk
- 2 teaspoons baking powder
- 1 teaspoon instant yeast
- 1 3/4 cups semolina
- 1/3 cup all purpose flour
- 1 teaspoon honey
- 1 teaspoon salt
- olive oil for cooking
- Merguez Filling
- 1 pound Merguez (spicy lamb sausage) either loose or in links, if using links cut into small pieces
- 1 small eggplant peeled and diced
- 1 small onion chopped
- 1/2- 1 teaspoons harissa paste
- 1 14.5 oz can fire roasted crushed tomatoes (I used muir glen)
- squeeze of fresh lemon
- salt and pepper to taste
- small handful flat leaf parsley chopped
- 1 cup greek yogurt (full fat is recommended but lowfat or fat free is fine)
- 2 tablespoons fresh mint finely chopped

Direction

- Pancakes
- In a bowl, combine 1/4 cup of the warm whey or water with the baking powder. In a food processor, combine the semolina with the flour, yeast, honey and the remaining 2 3/4 cups of warm water; process for 30 seconds, until smooth. Add the salt and baking powder mixture and process for 30 seconds longer. Pour the batter into a large bowl, cover with plastic wrap and a kitchen towel and let rise at room temperature until doubled in bulk, about 1 hour. I made this in the morning and let it rise for an hour then refrigerated until ready to make. Be sure to let it come to room temperature before making the pancakes.
- Heat a crepe pan or skillet coated with olive oil until it's hot, a drop of water should dance on the surface. Ladle some of the batter, it's fairly thin, into the pan and quickly spread so it makes a thin layer. Let it cook until bubbles appear then flip and brown on the other side. Keep in the oven on warm until ready to serve.
- Merguez Filling
- Make the yogurt and mint first and refrigerate, simply mix the plain yogurt with the mint, cover and place in refrigerator until ready to use. In a skillet heated with some olive oil add the onion and cook just until it starts to turn soft, add the eggplant and sauté until both are

lightly browned, add the merguez and cook with the onions and eggplant until its browned. If there is a lot of oil drain some out before adding the harissa and tomatoes. Add the harissa and stir to combine, now add the tomatoes and half can (use the can the tomatoes were in) of water (7 oz.). Cook on medium heat until it's thick, and reduced by half (about 20-30 minutes. Add a squeeze of fresh lemon juice and the chopped parsley. You judge how much harissa to use, it depends how spicy you like it and how spicy your merguez is.
- To serve: spoon some of the filling in a warm pancake, top with the yogurt and mint.

85. Sesame Semolina Pancakes

Serving: Serves 5 to 6 depends upon the size you choose to make | Prep: | Cook: | Ready in:

Ingredients

- 2 cups Semolina
- 1/2 cup Plain Yogurt
- 1/2 cup Water
- 1 tablespoon Ginger and green chillies paste
- 1 Green chilli Chopped optional if you prefer a little extra spice..
- Salt to taste
- 2 tablespoons Coriander leaves (if you do not like , just don't add them)
- 3 tablespoons Green Bell Pepper,thinly chopped
- 3 tablespoons Tomatoes, chopped
- 3 to 4 tablespoons Onions , thinly chopped
- 1/2 cup Oil
- 1 teaspoon Cumin seeds
- 1 teaspoon Mustard seeds
- 1 1/2 teaspoons White Sesame seeds

Direction

- Take the yogurt and whisk it and then add the water to it. If you have buttermilk, then replace it with yogurt and water mix. Mix in the ginger-chilli paste, salt and green chillies, and mix it well.
- Add the semolina and mix it nicely. Add a little water if you feel it is too thick. The batter should be not too thin and not too thick also.
- Finally, let it sit for about an hour or so or if you have time on hand for 2 hours or so. Lot of times I have made them without letting it sit, but what makes the difference is if you let it sit, the yogurt helps in fermenting the batter and making it a little more flavorful. Remember, semolina will use up the water once you let it sit.
- Whenever you are ready to prepare them, add in the chopped veggies and coriander leaves. Mix it well. At this point you might or might not feel like adding extra water. Do feel free to if you need to. Now, take the equal amount of mustard seeds, cumin seeds and sesame seeds in a bowl and mix them.
- Heat a skillet at medium high heat and add a small spoonful of oil about 1/2 tsp, add the cumin-mustard seeds-sesame seeds mix and be careful at this time the sesame seeds will go crazy and start popping up so quickly and might splatter on your face so please be careful and immediately pour in the batter on it top of the sesame mix and spread it a little like the way we make sweet pancakes. You can make them thin, if that's the way you like them or thick. It is totally up to you.
- Let them cook on one side , you will be able to see a difference on the batter once they look cooked on one side and then flip it on the other side, add a little oil to moisten it. Let it cook for about a minute or so and then remove it.
- Serve it hot off the griddle with some coriander/mint chutney.

86. Sfogliatelle

Serving: Makes 16 pastries | Prep: | Cook: | Ready in:

Ingredients

- DOUGH:
- 3 cups (361 g) all purpose flour
- 3/4 teaspoon (3 g) fine sea salt
- 6 ounces (170 g) unsalted butter, at room temperature
- 1 cup (237 g) room temperature water
- FOR ROLLING DOUGH
- 6 ounces (170 g) unsalted butter, at room temperature
- FILLING:
- 1 1/2 cups (356 g) whole milk
- 3/4 cup (149 g) granulated sugar
- 1 1/4 cups (204 g) semolina flour
- 3/4 teaspoon (3 g) fine sea salt
- 3 large (43 g) egg yolks
- 1 vanilla bean, halved and scraped
- zest of 1 lemon or orange (optional)
- pinch ground cardamom (optional)
- 2 cups (454 g) ricotta cheese
- 6 tablespoons (85 g) unsalted butter, melted
- powdered sugar, as needed for finishing

Direction

- Make the dough: in the bowl of an electric mixer fitted with the dough hook attachment, mix the flour, salt, butter, and water on low speed for 3 minutes. The dough should come together, but still look pretty rough. Raise speed to medium and mix for 3 minutes more—the dough should form a ball, but won't look totally smooth.
- Divide the dough in half. Use one right away, and wrap the other in plastic wrap. On a (very!) lightly floured surface, roll the first half into a rectangle about 5 x 10 inches.
- Set your pasta machine or rollers to the widest setting. Run the dough through the pasta machine, then fold it in half. Repeat this process 4 more times (a total of 5), continuing to run the folded dough through at the widest setting.
- Unwrap the second piece of dough, and use the plastic wrap to tightly wrap up the first piece (the dough will dry out if exposed too long to air in these early stages and become harder to work with). Repeat steps 2-3 with the second piece of dough.
- Unwrap the first piece of dough and place it on top of the second. Use a rolling pin to press the dough together, and roll it gently until it's about 1/2-inch thick.
- Run the dough through the pasta machine (still set to the widest setting), then fold it in half. Repeat a total of 10 times. After the final pass, fold the dough in half horizontally (from one long side to the other), then fold in half from one short side to the other.
- Wrap the dough tightly in plastic wrap and refrigerate for at least 1 1/2 hours.
- Quarter the dough—wrap all but one piece tightly in plastic wrap. On a (very!) lightly floured surface, roll out the dough into a rectangle about 4 x 7 inches. For the next step, you'll want to make sure you have access to a good amount of counter space, or maybe a friend or two to help (see headnote)!
- Set your pasta machine or rollers to the widest setting. Run the dough through the pasta machine. Flour the dough lightly as needed (I did not need to use flour at all for my dough). Continue passing the dough through the machine, making the setting smaller/narrower each time, until the dough is almost thin enough to see through—it will be about 4 feet long at this point. For me, this was the second to last setting on my pasta maker, but it may vary depending on yours!
- Gently lay the dough down on the counter. Working the length of the dough, gently stretch it to make it slightly wider and thinner (don't worry; it's very sturdy, but if you get a small rip or two, you won't be able to tell).
- Spread about 1/4 (1 1/2 ounces / 3 tablespoons) of the butter (listed under "for rolling the dough") of the butter in a thin, even layer across the dough. Starting from one of the short ends, roll the dough up into a tight spiral, leaving about 1 inch of dough unrolled up. Set aside, and cover loosely with plastic wrap.

- Repeat steps 8-10 with another quarter of the dough. Again, spread another 1/4 of the butter (1 1/2 ounces / 3 tablespoons) in a thin, even layer across the dough.
- Unwrap the first dough spiral that you rolled, and place the excess 1 inch of dough at the end of the new piece of dough, overlapping by about 1/4-inch. Continue to roll the spiral, now making the log even thicker by rolling up the whole length of the second piece of dough.
- The log should be about 2 inches thick and about 8 inches long. Wrap the log tightly in plastic wrap and refrigerate until firm, at least 2 hours and up to overnight.
- Repeat steps 8-14 with the remaining two pieces of dough.
- While the dough logs chill, make the filling. In a medium pot, stir the milk and sugar to combine. Bring to a simmer over medium heat. Once the milk begins to simmer, add the semolina in a slow, steady stream, stirring constantly (if needed, whisk the mixture to prevent lumps from forming).
- Continue to cook the mixture until it becomes thick, 1-2 minutes. Transfer to a parchment-lined baking sheet and spread into an even layer. Let cool completely.
- Transfer the semolina to the bowl of an electric mixer fitted with the whip attachment. Add the egg yolks, scraped vanilla bean seeds, the lemon or orange zest (if using), cardamom (if using, and the salt. Whip until the semolina begins to break up.
- Add the ricotta and mix until the mixture is well combined and relatively smooth. Cover with plastic wrap and refrigerate until ready to use.
- Preheat the oven to 400°F, and line two baking sheets with parchment paper.
- Remove the dough logs from the refrigerator and unwrap. Cut each log into 8 even pieces, about 1 inch thick. Working with one piece at a time, use your fingers (pressing to flatten between your fingers) to work your way around the edge of the dough, making it thinner. Continue the same motion, but work inward toward the center of the round. The idea is to make the whole piece of dough thinner but make it kind of cone shaped. As you work, you'll feel the layers in the dough, and it's almost as if you're fanning them out to create the final cone shape!
- Spoon about 2 tablespoons of filling into the center of the cone, fold it over so the ends meet, encasing the filling. Gently pinch the ends to seal. Transfer to the prepared baking sheet, and repeat with the remaining pieces of dough.
- Brush the surface of each pastry with melted butter, and bake until the pastries are very golden brown and crisp, 23-26 minutes. Rotate the trays front to back and between their racks halfway through baking, and brush with butter again.
- Let the pastries cool for at least 10 minutes, then dust generously with powdered sugar, and serve.

87. Sfoof Vegan Lebanese Yellow Tea Cake

Serving: Serves 16 | Prep: | Cook: | Ready in:

Ingredients

- 2 cups Semolina
- 1.5 cups All purpose flour
- 1 cup Almond Oil
- 2 teaspoons Turmeric
- 1 teaspoon Baking Powder
- 2 teaspoons Ground aniseed (can be substituted for 2 tsp of cardamom
- 1.5 cups Sugar
- 1.5 cups Soymilk (or water), chilled
- 2 tablespoons Tahini
- 1 handful Sesame seeds, slivered almonds or pine nuts, to garnish. I used chopped raw almonds

Direction

- Preheat the oven to 350°F (180°C)

- In a bowl, mix semolina, flour, turmeric, baking powder, and aniseed. Add oil and stir to make a runny paste.
- In a separate bowl, melt sugar in the chilled soymilk. Gradually beat the sugar mixture into the flour and spices paste.
- Grease the baking dish with tahini (or oil). Pour batter into the pan and ensure that the top is flat. Garnish with your choice of seeds or nuts.
- Bake for approximately 25 minutes, or until golden-brown. Insert a bamboo skewer into the cake; if it comes out clean, it's ready. Allow to cool for 10-15 minutes. Best served with tea or coffee.

88. Skinny Dip Squash (Butternut Gnudi)

Serving: Serves 4 (appetizers or first course) | Prep: | Cook: | Ready in:

Ingredients

- Gnudi
- 8 ounces Ricotta Cheese (Drained if Wet)
- 8 ounces Butternut Squash Puree (Roasted)
- 3 ounces Grated Parmesan or Pecorino Cheese
- 4 ounces Cake Flour (up to, may not use all)
- 1 Egg (Large)
- Brown Sugar (to taste depending on sweetness of squash puree)
- grated nutmeg
- ground cinnamon
- ground clove
- ground allspice
- 4 cups Semolina Flour
- Remaining Elements
- Apple Butter
- Heavy Cream
- 2 ounces Pancetta Chopped Coarse
- Seeds from 1 Butternut Squash
- 4 tablespoons Unsalted Butter
- Maple Syrup

Direction

- Season squash with spices to taste. I went heavier on nutmeg and cinnamon.
- Whisk together ricotta, parmesan, egg, and squash. Puree until smooth. Remove any clumps of squash.
- Gently mix in 2 ounces of cake flour, until the mixture seems sticky but workable. If the dough seems too sticky add an additional ounce at a time. The less flour the lighter the end product.
- Prepare a cookie sheet with a bed of semolina flour. This will go into the fridge overnight (so ensure it will fit in advance).
- Get a large bowl of cool water to rinse hands. Using a spoon or melon baller place a small amount of the dough in your hand. Working quickly, smooth dough into a ball. Then place on the prepared sheet pan. Rinsing hands in bowl between each gnudi.
- Cover prepared gnudi with additional semolina, and put in the fridge overnight.
- While gnudi are in fridge, I will bake squash seeds with a bit of olive oil at 350 degrees for 10 to 15 minutes. Until they color slightly. Then I drizzle the seeds with maple syrup and cook in a pan until candied/caramelized.
- The day you plan to serve the dish. Fry pancetta till crispy, and set aside.
- Mix apple butter with some heavy cream, until it can be effectively used in a squeeze bottle. Shaking the squeeze bottle will help to thicken mixture if to thin.
- Take Gnudi out of the fridge and remove from semolina. Based on what I have seen, you can reuse the semolina for a similar use shortly after (i.e. maybe pasta).
- Boil Water. Let gnudi warm, and using a spider gently place gnudi in the boiling water. Cook until they float or up to 1.5 minutes. Due to the heft of the squash, they may not fully float.
- Brown butter slightly in a pan.
- Plate as desired. As I mentioned I made a butternut squash outline of apple butter with brown butter inside. Placed the gnudi on top

of the brown butter, and piled the pancetta and candied squash seeds to the side. Garnish with a leaf (forced to use bay leaf, as I used up sage in squash ravioli this past weekend).
- Enjoy! Probably wish that you served as a dinner portion rather than appetizer.

89. Soda Bread With Walnuts And Rolled Oats

Serving: Serves 4-6 | Prep: | Cook: | Ready in:

Ingredients

- 1 cup rolled oats
- 1 cup whole wheat flour
- 1 cup unbleached white flour
- 1 cup semolina, or another cup of white or whole wheat flour, or a mix (NB if semolina is used, you may not need all the liquid)
- 1 teaspoon salt
- 1 teaspoon baking soda
- 2 teaspoons baking powder
- 2 cups buttermilk or yogurt thinned with milk or whole milk soured with lemon juice
- 1 handful walnuts broken up a bit with your fingers

Direction

- Preheat oven to 375.
- Mix up all the dry ingredients in a large bowl. You can play around with the grains a bit, but some whole wheat flour is important; I've used all whole wheat, which works, but makes it a bit heavier. Do use real rolled oats in all their chewy integrity, not quick cooking ones. Toss in the nuts when the flour, salt and leavening ingredients are well mixed up. I never actually measure the nuts, just keep breaking them into the bowl till it looks right.
- Add the acidulated dairy product slowly. Start with 1 and 1/2 cups, and stop when you have a workable dough. Especially if semolina is used - or other unusual flours, or if the buttermilk is unusually liquid - you may not need all of it. Stir, then mix with your hands to thoroughly incorporate the liquid. You can dump out on a floured board, but you don't have to. If you knead in the bowl, you can flour your hands and/or sprinkle the dough with a little flour if it looks too gloppy to touch at first. Be careful not to over mix, and knead as little as possible.
- Sprinkle a layer of rolled oats on the bottom of a dry cast iron pan or pie pan or baking sheet. Gather dough into a ball and drop it into the pan, forming it into a slightly flattened round shape. You need to cut into it to help it expand; the standard cut is a cross on top, but two slashes work as well.
- Put in oven and bake 45-50 minutes. Cool on rack, slice when no longer hot. Stays good for a few days.

90. Sooji Ka Halwa (A Sweet Made From Semolina)

Serving: Serves 8 | Prep: | Cook: | Ready in:

Ingredients

- 1 cup Semolina
- 3 cups Milk
- 1 1/2 cups Sugar
- 2 to 3 tablespoons Ghee (Clarified Butter)
- 1 teaspoon Cardamom powder
- Cashew Few
- Raisins few
- Food color one to two drop

Direction

- Roast Semolina until light brown.
- Boil the milk, add sugar, allow completely dissolve.
- Add roosted Semolina to the milk slowly, then add the ghee, cardamom powder and the food color Stir well for few minutes (until it resembles a thick porridge).

- Pour the Above porridge in a flat steel plate.
- Garnish with fried cashew and resins

91. Springtime Asparagus And Ricotta Pizza

Serving: Makes one 12-inch pizza | Prep: | Cook: | Ready in:

Ingredients

- 1 pound pizza dough (or half of Jim Lahey's No-Knead Pizza Dough recipe)
- 6 ounces fresh whole milk ricotta (about 3/4 cup)
- 1/2 cup balsamic vinegar
- 1/2 cup extra virgin olive oil
- 3 medium cloves garlic
- 4 teaspoons fresh thyme leaves
- 3 slices thick-cut applewood smoked bacon
- handful pencil asparagus (if using thicker asparagus split stalks lengthwise)
- 4 ounces grated Pecorino Romano (about 2 cups, loosely packed)
- freshly ground black pepper
- cornmeal or semolina (for dusting pizza peel or rimless baking sneet)

Direction

- Place pizza stone on oven rack in upper third of oven and preheat oven to 500° F. Oven should heat at least 30 minutes before cooking pizza. If pizza dough is refrigerated, bring to room temperature.
- Place a layer of paper towel in the bottom of a strainer, then add ricotta to strainer. Set aside.
- Steps 3, 4, and 5 can be done concurrently. Heat balsamic vinegar in a small pan or skillet over medium-high heat for about 15 minutes. Vinegar should reduce by more than half and become a syrup-like consistency. Set aside.
- Cut bacon slices crosswise into 1/4-inch strips. Fry in skillet over medium heat until most of fat has rendered out, and the bacon is starting to crisp. Drain bacon on paper towels, and set aside.
- Heat olive oil in small sauce pan over medium-low heat. Finely mince or press garlic and add to the oil. Once garlic starts to sizzle, remove from heat. Allow to cool for several minutes and add about 3/4 of the thyme leaves. Allow to infuse for several more minutes, then use immersion blender to combine. (You may need to transfer oil to a stick blender appropriate container to prevent oil from spattering everywhere.) Set aside.
- While completing steps 3, 4, and 5 remove tough ends from asparagus, and cut into approximately 1-inch lengths. Set aside. Coarsely chop remaining thyme leaves, and set aside.
- Form pizza dough into a 12 to 13 inch round. I like to work on a clean counter top. I first flatten it into a round using the palms of my hands. I then use my finger tips and work in a circular motion from the center to the edges pressing the dough down. I repeat this process several times until the dough is about 1/2-inch thick. Next I use one hand to hold the center of the dough, and the other hand to pull the edge of the dough outward working my way around the dough. After going around the dough a few times I cover it with damp paper towels and let it rest for 5 to 10 minutes to let it relax. I repeat the pulling until it has reached the desired diameter, then use my hands to press down the edges so they are only slightly thicker than the center of the dough.
- Dust your peel or baking sheet with semolina or corn meal. You don't want a thick layer, but need enough to prevent the dough from sticking. Carefully transfer the dough to the peel, and gently reform the circular shape if necessary.
- Brush the dough with the garlic-thyme olive oil. Grind some black pepper onto the crust. Sprinkle with about 3/4 of the pecorino. Scatter the bacon and asparagus over the cheese, leaving about a 1/2- to 3/4-inch border uncovered. Crumble the ricotta over

the bacon and asparagus. Sprinkle the remaining pecorino over the ricotta. Gently press ingredients to flatten slightly.
- Pull rack with pizza stone as far out of the oven as possible. Transfer pizza to stone using a quick jerking action to get the crust onto the back of the stone. Once part of the crust hits the stone, you can slide the peel out from under it. Slide rack back in, and bake pizza for 8 to 10 minutes, until the crust has risen, cheese is melted and crust and cheese are starting to brown.
- Remove pizza from oven. Drizzle with balsamic reduction and sprinkle with chopped thyme. Cut into wedges, serve immediately, and relish springtime!
- If you don't have a pizza stone you can bake the pizza on a sheet pan. Just place the oven rack in the center to bake it. Top the dough directly on the baking pan. Bake 10 to 12 minutes.

92. Sri Lankan Christmas Cake

Serving: Makes three 9x13 inch cake pans | Prep: | Cook: | Ready in:

Ingredients

- 1 pound cashew nuts, finely chopped
- 1 pound sultanas (golden raisins)
- 1 pound raisins (such as jumbo flames)
- 1 pound candied cherries
- One 16oz jar Sri Lankan ginger preserve (or 14 oz candied ginger)
- One 16oz jar Sri Lankan chow chow preserve (which, by the way, is not the same as Chinese, so do not substitute)
- 8 ounces Sri Lankan pumpkin preserve
- 1/2 pound candied orange peel
- 1/2 pound candied lemon peel
- 1 pound butter
- 1 pound semolina
- 24 egg yolks
- 12 egg whites
- 1 pound granulated sugar
- Zest of one lemon, finely shredded
- Zest of one orange, finely shredded
- Juice of one orange
- Juice of half lemon
- 3 tablespoons rose water
- 3 tablespoons vanilla extract
- 1 1/2 cups brandy (plus more for drizzling)
- 1/4 teaspoon ground nutmeg
- 1/2 teaspoon ground cinnamon
- 1/4 teaspoon ground cloves
- 1/8 teaspoon ground cardamom

Direction

- Open the preserve jars and drain the fruits from the syrup.
- Chop sultanas, raisins, candied fruits and fruits from the preserves into small pieces. Add the orange juice, lemon juice, brandy, half of the rose water and half of the vanilla extract. Mix well and leave in a jar for at least one day and up to three days.
- Beat the butter and sugar until creamy. Beat in the egg yolks. Add the orange zest, lemon zest and remaining rose water and vanilla extract, and continue to beat until combined. Add the semolina, nutmeg, cloves, cardamom and cinnamon and mix until well combined.
- Transfer the batter to a large bowl, add the brandied fruit mixture, and stir well until fruits and nuts are dispersed evenly throughout the batter.
- Beat the egg whites until stiff. Gently fold the whites into the cake batter.
- Preheat the oven to 250°F. Line three 13x9 inch cake pans with parchment paper. Turn the batter into the pans and bake for about 3 hours, until a toothpick inserted in the middle comes out clean. (Depending on the oven, the moisture level of your batter, etc. it might take longer, even up to 4 hours.)
- Let the cake cool in the pan for about 30min and then remove from the pan.
- Drizzle the cake with additional brandy and let it cool completely. Wrap the cake tightly in aluminum foil and store for at least a week

before serving. (The cake can be kept for a year in an airtight container. And you can keep on drizzling the brandy to keep it moist!)

93. Stinging Nettle Pasta

Serving: Serves 4 | Prep: | Cook: | Ready in:

Ingredients

- 2 cups all-purpose flour
- 2 cups semolina flour
- 2 eggs
- 3 egg yolks
- 1 cup blanched stinging nettles, finely chopped
- 1 teaspoon salt
- 1 tablespoon water
- 1 tablespoon olive oil
- Extra flour for dusting

Direction

- In a large mixing bowl combine the flour and semolina.
- Add the rest of the ingredients into a blender and blend quickly to combine. You don't want it to emulsify, but the nettles should be well incorporated.
- Add the mixture from the blender to the bowl and stir well to combine.
- Once the dough has begun to come together, find a clean surface and dust with flour. Knead the dough by hand for 5 minutes to develop the gluten, adding more water or flour as needed.
- Wrap in plastic or place in a Ziploc bag and chill for at least 30 minutes before rolling out. Roll out to whatever size or shape you like, either by hand or according to your pasta machine's directions.

94. Summer Squash With Saffron Fettuccine

Serving: Serves 2-4 | Prep: | Cook: | Ready in:

Ingredients

- Saffron Fettuchine
- 10-15 threads saffron
- 1/4 cup warm water
- 2 best freshest eggs
- 2 cups "00" flour
- 1 Pinch fine salt
- hadnfull or so of semolina flour or if you have to, all purpose
- Summer Squash
- 3 or 4 cloves garlic
- 10 threads saffron soaked in hot water (optional)
- 1 cup chicken or vegetable stock
- 1 tablespoon lemon zest
- 1/4 cup white wine
- squeeze fresh lemon
- 1/4 cup olive oil
- pinch red pepper flakes
- 2 cups assorted summer squashes, julienned
- 6-7 squash blossoms
- 1 tablespoon fresh basil (purple if you can find it)
- handful pecorino cheese
- 1 tablespoon fresh mint
- nasturtiums if you can find them

Direction

- Saffron Fettuccine
- Soak saffron threads in 2 tablespoons of hot water.
- Put flour on clean surface or in a very large bowl. Lacking clean surfaces (I have naughty cats), well surfaces in general (no counter space), I use a HUGE stainless steel mixing bowl.
- Make a little well in the center of the flour, it should look sort of like flat wide volcano.
- Whisk the saffron water and salt into the eggs.

- Pour the eggs in to the well in the center and start mixing around with your index and middle finger, slowing pulling in the flour from the sides of the walls. Letting it collapse into itself slowly. If it is too stiff, you can add dribbles of warm water till it all comes together.
- Once it has come together, knead gently but firmly, you'll feel the gluten come together as you work the dough, it will become smooth and shiny and more elastic (I love that part).
- Shape into a disk and refrigerate for an hour.
- Remove dough from fridge cut into 8 quarters with a plastic pastry cutter or really whatever you have, if you have someone helping you on a long table you can cut it in fourths. I have a strange dance and drape thing I have to do rolling out the dough.
- Set pasta roller on 1. Roll out 1 section, fold it in thirds, roll it out again, fold it in thirds roll it out again. Now set to 2, and roll it out, then move to 3... Keep going until you get to 7.
- If you have the attachment that makes fettuccine, cut the pasta after it's gone through 7. If you don't you can lay the pasta sheets out on a parchment & semolina covered sheet tray and cut them yourself with a sharp knife. If you like things to be perfect you can use a ruler as a guide, they should be about 8 inches long.
- Cover each layer with parchment paper to keep them from drying out too much.
- Before boiling give the pasta a bit of a "juzdge" to make sure they don't stick together.
- Summer Squash
- Put on a pot of heavily salted water for pasta.
- Slice garlic and sweat in olive oil till just translucent. DON'T let it brown. Add half the lemon zest, the chicken stock, wine and saffron and let it reduce by half. If you'll like this on the spicy side add red pepper flakes now, otherwise save to garnish at the end or leave out altogether.
- While sauce is reducing, julienne the squash blossoms reserving 1 for garnish, you don't want them to sit very long cut or they will wilt too quickly. Taste and season remembering that you will be adding salt via the pasta water and cheese.
- Once sauce has reduced add blossoms and squash to sauce, stir around, keeping flame low, cover and drop pasta in to boiling water.
- Drop pasta and give it a good stir, should take no more than 3-4 minutes until it's done. Remove and reserve a ladleful of water before draining pasta.
- Add pasta to sauce and stir until completely coated. Add the pasta water, plus 2 tablespoons of cheese, plus the reserved uncut blossom. Heat and let cook another 2 minutes so the pasta has the opportunity to absorb the sauce.
- Remove from heat, add fresh herbs and remaining cheese, a bit of fresh ground pepper and toss well. Find the whole squash blossom and put it on top. Additional garnishes: edible flowers and purple basil if you have them.

95. Trick To Rolling Out Homemade Pasta Dough!

Serving: Serves 4 | Prep: | Cook: | Ready in:

Ingredients

- 7 ounces (200 grams) of Italian tipo 00 flour
- 3.5 ounces (100 grams) of semolina flour
- 1/2 teaspoon fine salt
- 3 large free-range eggs

Direction

- To make the dough: Place all the flours and salt inside a large bowl and make a well in the center. Add the large egg yolks (or whole eggs) into the center of the well and whisk them with a fork. Slowly work your way outwards to gradually incorporate the flour into the eggs. Now slowly knead the dough inside the bowl and try to get all the flours into the dough. If the dough feel too dry to come together, wet your hands with water and work the water into the dough (instead of pouring water directly onto the dough) because it gives you better control as how much more water you are adding. Once the dough as come together, take it out of the bowl and start kneading on the counter. You must do this vigorously for about 10 minutes, until the dough is very smooth and elastic. It should spring back when you make a dent with your finger. Wrap the dough in plastic wrap and let rest for at least 30 min.

- To roll out the dough: Dust the counter with semolina flour and place the dough on top. Cut the dough in half and cover 1 piece under plastic wrap.
- With the other piece of dough, dust lightly with semolina flour and press it down into a flat oval shape with your hands. With a counter-top pasta machine, or a pasta machine-attachment on your mixer, run the dough through the widest setting. Then fold the dough in 3 folds (like folding a letter), and run it again. Repeat once more.
- Now you should have a rectangular/oval-shaped dough with sort of uneven ends. Don't worry about it. Feed the dough through the machine again, but this time, STOP MIDWAY. Then bring the 2 ends of the dough together, overlap them and pinch them lightly so they stick. Hold them in position and start running it again through the machine. Once the "seam" passes through the machine, you should have a connected, "conveyor belt" looking pasta sheet that passes through the machine. Keep running the machine to ensure that the seam/connection point is tightly merged together. Now, no more re-feeding.
- All you have to do now is setting the machine to the next increment, and keep the pasta sheet rolling through it (like a conveyor belt!). Make sure to dust generously with flour on top AND underneath, and that the entire length of the pasta sheet has passed through each increment before moving onto the next. Roll the pasta sheet out to your desired thickness, then sever it midway. Roll the pasta sheet out of the machine to release it. And cut into desired shape. Repeat with the other half of the pasta dough.

96. Vegetable Stuffed Snack Cakes

Serving: Serves 6–8 | Prep: | Cook: | Ready in:

Ingredients

- 1 cup (120g) coarse semolina flour
- 1/2 cup (60g) chickpea flour
- 1 cup (240g) yogurt
- 1/4 cup (60ml) olive oil
- 1 tablespoon (8g) baking powder, divided
- 2 teaspoons (12g) salt, divided
- 1 tablespoon (15ml) fresh lemon juice
- 1 small carrot
- 1 small onion
- 1 red bell pepper
- 2 tablespoons (28g) ghee
- 1 teaspoon cumin seeds
- 1 teaspoon mustard seeds
- 1 teaspoon asafetida
- 1 inch (2.5cm) piece ginger, grated
- 3 green chiles, finely chopped
- 1/2 cup (70g) peas
- 1/2 cup (40g) shredded cabbage
- 1/2 cup (8g) cilantro
- 1/4 cup (60ml) warm water
- 1/3 cup (43g) sesame seeds

Direction

- Preheat the oven to 375°F (190°C, or gas mark 5). Grease a 9-inch (23-cm) springform cake pan, mini tart pans or muffin tins. Alternatively, you can steam this.
- In a sauté pan, fry the semolina flour over medium heat for 2 minutes, or until it's a pale golden color. Do not brown it too much. Add the chickpea flour and toast it for 2 minutes, until you smell a nutty aroma. Turn off the heat and transfer the flours to a mixing bowl. Set aside.

- In a small mixing bowl, combine the yogurt, olive oil, ½ tablespoon (4 g) of the baking powder, 1 1/2 teaspoons (9 g) of the salt and lemon juice. Mix well and let it sit while you get the vegetables ready.
- Peel the carrot and onion and dice them finely. Dice the bell pepper (or use a food processor). Combine the toasted flours and remaining 1/2 tablespoon (4 g) baking powder in a large bowl. Add the yogurt mixture and blend well.
- Warm the ghee in a pan over medium heat. Add the cumin seeds, mustard seeds, asafetida, grated ginger and finely chopped chiles. Sauté for a few minutes, then add the chopped vegetables, peas, cabbage, cilantro and the remaining 1/2 teaspoon salt and cook just for a couple of minutes; the vegetables should still be crunchy. Turn off the heat and let it cool completely.
- Once the veggies are completely cooled, add them to the semolina mixture and blend everything well. The batter should be thick. Check for salt. Add the warm water to the batter and mix thoroughly with a wooden spoon.
- Pour the batter into the prepared pan(s). Sprinkle generously with the sesame seeds. Bake in the center of the oven for 15 minutes, then reduce the temperature to 300°F (150°C, or gas mark 2) and bake for 45 to 60 minutes longer for a large cake or 20 to 25 minutes longer for mini tarts or muffins. Alternatively, you can pour some water into a deep wok, place a stand inside, pour the batter into a 9-inch (23-cm) springform pan, cover and steam for 20 to 25 minutes.
- The cake is ready when it is a dark brown color and a toothpick inserted into the center comes out clean. Remove from the oven and cool in the pan for 30 minutes. Take the cake out of the pan, cut into slices and serve warm or cold. This is delicious with a green chutney, pesto or any sauce.

97. Vermicelli And Semolina Idli

Serving: Serves 6 | Prep: | Cook: | Ready in:

Ingredients

- Semolina /Sooji - 1 cup Vermicelli /sevai - 1 cup Yogurt /dahi - 1 cup Green chili, chopped - 1 tsp French beans, finely chopped- 2 tbsp Carrot ,finely chopped- 2 tbsp Ginger,finely chopped -1 tsp Turmeric- a pinch of (optional) Fruit salt/eno- 1tsp Salt-

Direction

- Heat oil in a pan and add white lentil and sauté.
- When it becomes pink then add mustard seeds and cashews.
- When seed start crackling then add vermicelli and sauté on medium heat for 2 minutes.
- Now add semolina, green chilies and curry leaves and roast for a minute.
- Switch off the flame, add chopped vegetables and let it cool down completely.
- Now add beaten yogurt, salt and some water and make a medium thick batter.
- Cover and rest for 20 minutes.
- Grease idli molds and boil water in the steamer.
- When water start boiling then add eno in the batter and fill in the idli molds.
- Steam for 10 minutes in the steamer.
- Take out, rest for 2 minutes and scoop out with a wet spoon.
- Serve with coconut chutney and tomato chutney.

98. Weeknight Margeritesque Pizza

Serving: Makes two medium pizzas or one large pizza | Prep: | Cook: | Ready in:

Ingredients

- 1 packet yeast
- 2 tablespoons honey
- 3/4 cup warm water
- 3/4 cup semolina flour
- 1 cup all-purpose flour
- 2 teaspoons salt
- 1 cup watercress, roughly chopped
- 1/4 cup basil
- 1/4 cup olive oil
- 1/4 cup pine nuts
- 1/4 cup pecorino romano
- 1 cup crushed tomatoes (preferably from san marzano)
- 1 small shallot, chopped
- 2 ounces goat cheese
- cracked black pepper
- 1/4 pound asparagus, chopped
- 1/2 cup mushrooms, sliced
- 4-6 ounces fresh mozzarella, sliced and drained

Direction

- Preheat oven to 550° with a pizza stone on the center rack.
- Combine yeast, honey, and water in a large bowl or the bowl of a stand mixer fitted with a dough hook. Let rest 5-10 minutes.
- Meanwhile, combine watercress, basil, olive oil, pine nuts, and pecorino in a blender or food processor. Puree until slightly chunky. Set aside.
- Combine semolina, all-purpose flour, and salt in a bowl. With a wooden spoon, or in the stand mixer on low speed, slowly add half the flour, mixing until incorporated. Begin mixing more vigorously until the mixture begins to look stringy. Slowly add the rest of the flour and mix until well combined. The mixture should be slightly tacky, but not wet. Add extra water or flour 1 teaspoon at a time until it reaches this consistency.
- Turn the dough onto a lightly floured board and knead for 2-3 minutes. Divide into 2 pieces, rolling each into tight balls. Cover with a dampened cloth and set aside.
- In a small bowl, combine tomatoes, shallot, and 1 T salt. (The crushed tomatoes I buy are very thick, about the consistency of tapenade or homemade ketchup--if yours are more watery, you may need to cook them down a bit.) Set aside.
- In a small bowl, combine goat cheese with 1 T crushed black pepper.
- Sauté asparagus and mushrooms in a medium skillet over medium-high heat until the asparagus is bright green and the mushrooms are just beginning to brown.
- Assemble the pizza: Cover a pizza peel with a sheet of parchment paper. Sprinkle the paper lightly with semolina. Either hand-stretch or roll out the pizza to about 12" diameter. Spread 1/4 - 1/2 cup of the tomato sauce. Scatter mozzarella and dollops of goat cheese and pesto. Top with asparagus and mushrooms.
- Slide pizza and parchment onto the baking stone, and cook for 6-9 minutes, or until cheese is bubbling and crust is golden brown. Let rest 2-3 minutes before cutting. Repeat with second pizza.

99. Zapekanka, A Classic Breakfast Dish From Russian Cuisine

Serving: Makes 1(9-by-5-inches) loaf | Prep: | Cook: | Ready in:

Ingredients

- • 4 extra-large eggs, room temperature
- • 1/2 cup organic cane sugar
- • 2 1/2 cups whole milk Farmer's cheese or well drained Ricotta
- • 1/2 teaspoon kosher or sea salt
- • 1/2 cup sour cream mixed with ½ teaspoon of baking soda and ½ teaspoon of lemon juice
- • Zest of 1 large orange or lemon
- • 2 teaspoons pure vanilla extract or 1/2 teaspoon of Fiori de Sicilia* extract

- • 2 heaping tablespoons semolina (Cream of Wheat, Farina)
- • About 1/4 cup of each: chopped candied orange or other citrus peel, mini chocolate chips and chopped dried berries or fruit soaked in rum or brandy

Direction

- Preheat the oven to 325 degrees F. Butter a 9-by 5-inches loaf pan; then line the bottom with parchment paper, and butter the parchment paper also.
- In a mixing bowl, beat the eggs and sugar until light, fluffy and pale yellow, about 8 to 10 minutes.
- In another large bowl whisk Farmer's cheese or Ricotta, salt, sour cream mixture, orange zest and vanilla until very smooth and well combined.
- Slowly add the egg and sugar mixture until fully incorporated; then mix in the semolina. Using a rubber spatula, fold in the candied citrus peel, mini chocolate chips and the soaked and drained fruit or berries.
- Let the batter rest for about 20 to 30 minutes. This step allows the semolina to absorb the excess moisture and swell in the batter.
- Evenly spread the batter in the prepared loaf pan, transfer to the middle rack of the oven and bake for about 40-50 minutes, until the cake is golden brown and doesn't jiggle in the center. When the cake is done, allow it to cool in the pan for about 20 minutes on a wire rack. Then run a paring knife around the edges and carefully invert to a serving platter.
- * An Italian favorite, Fiori di Sicilia is excellent in sweet dishes that allow the complex flavor and aroma to truly shine. The dominant flavors in Fiori di Sicilia are vanilla and orange, so a combination of those two make a fine substitute. Also a little rose flower water, if you can find some of that, will make up for some of the floral aromas.

100. Roasted Semolina Soup

Serving: Serves 4 | Prep: | Cook: | Ready in:

Ingredients

- 125 grams wheat semolina
- 500 milliliters milk
- 500 milliliters vegetable or chicken stock
- 1 egg yolk
- 1 generous dash of freshly ground nutmeg

Direction

- Melt butter, add semolina and roast over medium to high heat, stirring constantly with a wooden spoon, until the grains are sandy, slightly browned, and have a nice smell. Stay by the pot, as the semolina burns fast.
- Pour stock, stir well, reduce the heat to low, add milk, and allow to simmer for 5-10 minutes, stirring frequently.
- Season with ground nutmeg.
- Stir in the egg yolk.
- Serve as it is, or add a handful chunks of fried bacon and chopped parsley.

101. Semolina With Red Fruit Topping

Serving: Serves 20 | Prep: | Cook: | Ready in:

Ingredients

- 1 cup Fine semolina
- 1 cup Sugar
- 6 cups Milk
- 150 milliliters Fresh cream
- Vanilla
- 500 grams Fresh or frozen strawberries or mixed soft red fruits(raspberries strawberries)
- 1/2 cup Sugar
- 1 cup Crushed almonds. (Small bits)

Direction

- Put the fruit in a blender and blend until there are no lumps. Add the sugar and boil for app 10 minutes. Cool.
- Pour milk, sugar and semolina in a pan and heat stirring continually. When it boils, take it off the heat and stir in the fresh cream, vanilla and nuts.
- Pour it immediately in a glass serving dish, oval or round approx. 35cmm long and at least 8cmm high.

Index

A
Almond 3,5,9,19,52,70

Anchovies 3,32

Apple 71

Apricot 3,47

Asparagus 4,73

B
Baking 7,8,12,19,41,42,43,49,50,62,70

Basil 3,10,27,28

Beetroot 3,11

Blueberry 3,4,12,58

Bran 3,13

Bread 3,4,13,24,25,31,32,36,55,56,72

Broccoli 3,14,30

Buckwheat 3,15

Butter 3,4,11,12,16,17,18,24,41,44,46,56,57,59,71,72,80

C
Cabbage 3,15

Cake 3,4,5,9,13,23,41,42,51,57,58,65,70,71,74,77

Caramel 3,23

Cardamom 3,4,19,20,52,53,72

Carrot 3,4,19,20,59,78

Cashew 72

Cauliflower 3,20

Celery 3,31

Cheese 3,4,11,40,66,71

Chicken 3,7

Chickpea 19

Chilli 62

Chocolate 3,26

Chutney 62

Cinnamon 3,21

Clarified butter 20,52

Coconut 3,4,22,32,36,51,53,62

Condensed milk 20,51

Coriander 68

Crackers 4,66

Cream 3,27,38,41,58,59,62,71,80

Crumble 73

Cumin 3,20,26,43,68

Curry 3,32

Custard 3,27,39

D
Date 3,4,5,44,45,53

Dijon mustard 8

Dumplings 3,4,47,66

E
Egg 8,12,21,63,71

English muffin 29

F
Farfalle 3,37

Feta 4,59,60

Fettuccine 4,75

Flank 3,35

Flour 8,19,21,30,36,42,52,69,71

French beans 78

Fruit 3,4,13,48,78,80

G
Garlic 3,17

Ghee 36,46,52,72

Gin 3,33,68,78

Gnocchi 4,58,59

Gorgonzola 3,16

Gram flour 20,52
Grapes 15

H

Hazelnut 3,47
Honey 3,27,39,48

I

Icing 34

J

Jus 25,47,50,74

K

Kale 3,40

L

Lemon 3,4,9,12,26,32,38,59,63
Lentils 3,43

M

Mango 3,46
Maple syrup 12
Mascarpone 21
Milk 4,8,9,19,44,52,53,60,72,80
Mince 53
Mozzarella 3,49
Muffins 3,12,29
Mustard 68

N

Nettle 4,60,75

O

Oats 4,72
Oil 8,62,68,70
Olive 3,43,47,49,56
Onion 3,13,27,28,68
Orange 3,26,41,51

P

Pancakes 3,4,7,23,52,61,67,68
Pancetta 71
Pappardelle 3,10
Parmesan 6,7,20,21,34,67,71
Pasta 3,4,10,15,18,21,27,28,30,31,38,53,75,76
Pastry 17,36
Peach 4,54
Peanuts 62
Peas 4,59
Pecorino 14,15,55,71,73
Peel 6,12,18,65,78
Pepper 3,8,10,27,28,29,68
Pesto 3,27,28
Pickle 3,31
Pie 3,4,33,54
Pineapple 52
Pistachio 19,41,45,52,63
Pizza 3,4,14,15,28,40,56,73,78
Plum 3,23
Poppy seeds 41
Port 3,51
Potato 3,14,25
Prosciutto 3,49
Pulse 17,18,36

Q

Quark 47,48
Quinoa 3,22,40

R

Raisins 3,30,52,72
Rice 3,52
Ricotta 3,4,6,7,11,12,58,59,71,73,79,80
Rosemary 3,4,14,59
Rosewater 3,9

S

Saffron 3,4,5,41,52,75

Sage 3,18

Salad 3,49

Salt 6,10,14,15,19,20,31,32,35,43,47,52,55,60,62,63,68,78

Sausage 3,27,28,30

Savory 4,65

Sea salt 8

Seeds 43,71

Semolina 1,3,4,5,7,8,9,10,12,18,19,20,21,26,29,41,42,43,44,46,52,56, 57,58,61,63,66,67,68,70,71,72,78,80

Sesame seeds 68,70

Shin 33

Shortbread 3,20,44,45

Soda 4,72

Soup 3,4,29,47,59,80

Spinach 3,21,38

Squash 3,4,16,17,18,56,71,75,76

Steak 3,35

Stew 4,64

Sugar 3,7,8,20,36,41,44,46,51,52,62,63,70,71,72,80

Syrup 3,4,9,39,53,57,61,71

T

Tagliatelle 3,21

Tahini 70

Tamari 62

Tea 4,33,70

Tomato 4,54,68

Turmeric 20,70,78

V

Vegan 4,70

Vegetable oil 7

Vinegar 73

W

Walnut 3,4,11,40,45,72

Worcestershire sauce 35

Y

Yeast 52

Z

Zest 13,15,31,60,74,79

Conclusion

Thank you again for downloading this book!

I hope you enjoyed reading about my book!

If you enjoyed this book, please take the time to share your thoughts and post a review on Amazon. It'd be greatly appreciated!

Write me an honest review about the book – I truly value your opinion and thoughts and I will incorporate them into my next book, which is already underway.

Thank you!

If you have any questions, **feel free to contact at:** author@shellfishrecipes.com

Alice Grady

shellfishrecipes.com

Printed in Great Britain
by Amazon